The Honor and Dignity of the Profession

THE HONOR & DIGNITY OF THE PROFESSION

A History of the Mississippi State Bar, 1906–1976

MICHAEL DE L. LANDON

PUBLISHED FOR THE
MISSISSIPPI BAR FOUNDATION
BY THE
UNIVERSITY PRESS OF MISSISSIPPI
JACKSON • 1979

Library of Congress Cataloging in Publication Data

Landon, Michael.
The honor and dignity of the profession.

Includes bibliographical references and index.
1. Mississippi State Bar—History. I. Title.
KF332.M56M564 340'.06'2762 79-4317
ISBN 0-87805-101-5

Dedicated to

N. W. Overstreet, Jr.

Table of Contents

Preface

THE CELEBRATION of the bicentennial anniversary of the Republic in 1976 caused most Americans to pause and reflect not only on their national history but also on the roots and backgrounds of their particular regions, states, localities, ethnic groups, churches, and professional organizations. The directors and fellows of the Mississippi Bar Foundation were of course especially interested in the history of the organized bar in the state, and so they commissioned the writing of this book. What is provided in the following pages is not a final and definitive history of the Mississippi State Bar in the first three quarters of the twentieth century. Before such a work can be written much more research needs to be done; and I would suggest to my colleagues teaching history in the state's universities that there is material for several masters theses, and even a doctoral dissertation or two, in connection with the topic. Meanwhile, it is hoped that this short, overall account of the major issues, events, and personalities in the history of the Bar Association during the past seven decades will be of some interest to all Mississippians who enjoy reading about their state's colorful past and of particular interest to the lawyers of Mississippi whose own organizational history it is.

My thanks go to the two immediate past-presidents of the Bar Foundation, Thomas R. Ethridge and Frank D. Montague, Jr., for their patience, encouragement, and assistance during the past eighteen months. Thanks are also due to several members of the Bar; Frank E. Everett, Jr., John C. Satterfield, Lucy S. Howorth, Parham H. Williams, E. Grady Jolly, Jr., and E. Clifton Hodge, Jr. all provided me with useful information. Fred Smith, Hugh Clayton, and Robert Farley very kindly consented to be interviewed on tape concerning their memories of the Bar Association over several decades. I was also helped by Mrs. Louise LeCroy Dubard of Booneville who made available to me information on the early women graduates of the University of Mississippi Law School that I was unable to obtain elsewhere.

Dr. Thomas Verich, the University of Mississippi archivist, and his predecessor, Dr. Ed Walters, have both been of great help as have all of the staff of the University Library's Mississippi Collection. My thanks also go to Professor James Cooke and other colleagues in the history department here who have aided me in one way or another, and to my wife, Doris, one of the newest members of the State Bar, for her patient assistance. Above all, I am grateful to Webb Overstreet, a trustee and former President of the Bar Foundation who has worked with me on this project, for his valuable suggestions and corrections; to George Van Zant, Executive Director of the State Bar, for making his records available to me and assisting me with a great deal of information; and to my colleague, Dr. David Sansing, whose advice, based on a profound knowledge of Mississippi history and a great talent for writing it, has been invaluable at every stage of this project.

Michael de L. Landon
University, Mississippi
August, 1978

A Note on Sources

MOST of the information for this book was derived from the published proceedings of the annual meetings of the Bar. From 1906 to 1927 the proceedings were printed and distributed each year in booklet form (referred to in the footnotes as *Proc.*). From 1928 to 1971 they were printed in the fall issue of the *Mississippi Law Journal.* In order to avoid overburdening the book with footnotes, references to statements made or events occurring at annual meetings are not footnoted. Except where there is a footnote indicating otherwise, it can be assumed that the source for them is the published proceedings of the meeting being discussed. Full bibliographical information on all other published sources is given in the first footnote in which they are cited except for the *General Laws of Mississippi*, which are abbreviated throughout as *Miss. Laws*, and the *Mississippi Law Journal*, which is abbreviated throughout as *Miss. LJ*.

The Honor and Dignity of the Profession

I

Mississippi's Third State Bar Association

1906

On January 4, 1906, at four o'clock in the afternoon, "pursuant to the call of certain attorneys at law, members of the Legislature . . . then sitting," a meeting of lawyer-legislators was held in the Hall of the House of Representatives in Mississippi's "New Capitol Building."[1] Hardin H. Brooks, one of the representatives from Noxubee County, was called upon to preside over the gathering, and Senator G. Wood Magee from Lawrence County acted as secretary. Sydney M. Smith, a representative from Holmes County who would soon be commissioned as the circuit judge for the fourth district, opened the proceedings with "a short address, setting forth the objects of the meeting." He was followed at the podium by T. C. Catchings, a former state attorney general (1878–1886). Then two jurists who intended to run for governor in 1907 were heard from: T. U. Sisson from Montgomery County and E. F. Noel from Holmes County. All three delivered "forcible addresses" of which unfortunately no record was kept. But when they had finished speaking, Representative W. B. Mixon from Pike County moved a resolution that "it is the desire of the practicing lawyers who are members of the Senate and House of Representatives of Mississippi that a Bar Association of the State of Mississippi be organized. . . ." The motion passed.

There had been two earlier state bar associations in Mississip-

1. *Proc.* (1906), p. 7. The new state capitol building had been dedicated on June 3, 1903. The 1906 session of the Legislature had convened just two days earlier, on January 2.

pi's history. The first, founded in 1821 at Natchez, had continued to exist until 1825. It apparently represented an attempt by the established leaders of the bar to maintain some sort of professional standards in a frontier situation where newcomers were arriving on the scene daily, many of them claiming to be trained attorneys. The inability of the members to agree as to just what those standards ought to be was a major cause of the organization's breaking up after just a few years of active life.[2] The spirit of Jacksonian Democracy was hostile to exclusive professional groups in the mid-nineteenth century; and the stormy events and strong passions of the Civil War and Reconstruction periods continued to make organized cooperation difficult. But by 1885 there was talk of a new state constitution for Mississippi; and the second bar association organized in 1886 apparently came into being because of a desire on the part of the lawyers to have some say in its formulation, especially with regard to the judicial branch. The adoption in 1890 of the new constitution, which included very few changes in the judiciary, of course removed that motivation. So the new organization, like its predecessor seven decades earlier, dwindled and died. The published reports of its proceedings end with 1892. Meetings were held in 1893 and 1894, but the latter was "poorly attended," and after it there were no more.[3]

By the end of the nineteenth century, however, the climate of opinion in America had changed in favor of bar associations at the local, state, and national levels. The final completion of a nationwide system of railroads that made long distance travel easier and faster undoubtedly was one factor that encouraged the trend towards fellow professionals getting together. Another was the growing desire on the part of many of the better educated and more progressive American lawyers to copy the example of England where the Judiciary Act of 1873 had been but the first of a num-

---

2. For some notes on the first association and the minutes of its proceedings, see Mississippi Bar Foundation, *Early Mississippi Bar Associations* (Jackson, 1966), pp. 5–20, 25–46.

3. *Proceedings*, 1886–1892 *passim*. Carrol C. Moreland, "Check List of State Bar Association Proceedings," *Law Library Journal*, LXIII (1969), 142.

ber of important measures of judicial and legal reform. Finally, the development of a continent-sized, national economic and trading system had made it seem very desirable to work towards greater uniformity in the legal codes of the various states, particularly with regard to matters of banking and commerce. Organized groups of lawyers were obviously best able to lobby for such reforms and innovations.

The American Bar Association was organized at Saratoga Springs, New York, in 1878. By then both New York (1876) and Illinois (1877) already had state bar associations which have continued in existence to the present. The move to create them undoubtedly had originated in America's two mighty commercial metropolises, New York City and Chicago. Mississippi lawyers from the very first were active in the A.B.A. In fact at its organizational meeting in 1878 only Massachusetts, Pennsylvania, and New York had larger delegations present.[4] And the A.B.A. encouraged the creation of state associations which would send official delegations to the national organization's annual meetings. By the end of 1905, in fact, Mississippi was one of a very tiny minority of states that did not have an active state bar organization. Forty of the then forty-five states did, and so did the territories of Oklahoma and New Mexico and the District of Columbia.[5]

Quite apart from the national trend, however, many Mississippi lawyers were also influenced by in-state considerations in their desire for an organized bar in 1906. The established, ruling elite of the state—the big plantation owners and their relatives and associates, including many leading attorneys—felt threatened by the election to the governorship in 1903 of James Kimble Vardaman, a flamboyant newspaperman, editor, and attorney from Greenwood, whose political appeals to poor-white sentiments and interests caused him to be labelled a "populist" and a "radical." Ac-

4. J. C. Satterfield, "What Can Bar Associations Do For Lawyers?" *Miss. LJ*, XXXII (1960–61), 341.

5. Lawrence M. Friedman, *A History of American Law* (New York: Simon and Schuster, 1973), pp. 355, 363. Philip J. Wickser, "Bar Associations," *Cornell LJ*, XV (1929–30), 417. Wickser incorrectly dates Mississippi's two 19th century associations as 1825 and 1892–96.

cording to one of his political opponents, the governor was both "vulgar and dangerous." A majority in the legislature, whose lawyer members took the first steps in 1906 towards organizing the new bar association, were strongly opposed to him and his leveling policies. An organized bar would obviously be able to oppose those policies more effectively.[6]

The leader of the conservative element in state politics at the time was Anselm J. McLaurin, a former governor (1896–1900) who had since been elected to the United States Senate. In 1905 he and Vardaman had engaged in a confrontation over the "Sandy Bayou" affair. Although the new constitution of 1890 prohibited the leasing out of state convicts as cheap labor to private landowners, penitentiary board members and their planter friends had soon devised an alternative system whereby the board leased plantation lands and worked them with convict labor on a sharecropping basis that was even more profitable to the owners than the old system had been. Since the independently elected attorney-general, William Williams, declined to take any action in the matter, Vardaman himself challenged the constitutionality of the new scheme in the state courts. Specifically he asked that the penitentiary board be enjoined from leasing a large tract of the Sandy Bayou plantation in Sharkey County which belonged to Senator McLaurin's brother, H. H. McLaurin.

Hinds County chancellor, Robert B. Mayes, agreed to issue an injunction; and, when the matter was appealed to the state Supreme Court, Chief Justice A. H. Whitfield, who had been reappointed to the court by Vardaman, supported Mayes' decision. But the two other Supreme Court justices, Solomon Saladin Calhoun of Jackson and Jeff Truly of Fayette, who had been appointed by McLaurin's political ally, Governor A. H. Longino (1900–1904), in their majority decision ruled that the lease in question

6. Albert D. Kirwan, *The Revolt of the Rednecks* (Gloucester, Mass.: Peter Smith, 1964), pp. 103–21, 158–61, 193. R. A. McLemore (ed.), *A History of Mississippi* (2 vols.; Hattiesburg: University and College Press of Mississippi, 1973), II, 32, 36–37.

was of land not of convicts and that, furthermore, the governor was not empowered to bring any kind of suit in the name of the state. In a second decision, handed down late in 1905, the same two justices refused a request by Vardaman for a *Mandamus* that would have returned the convicts in question to state control.[7] The governor did triumph in the end, however. One of the few measures he advocated that the 1906 session of the Legislature went along with was the passage of an act making it illegal to employ convict labor on any but state-owned lands.[8]

Another major legislative concern in that same session was the enactment of what would be Mississippi's thirteenth new code of laws. The regular session of 1904 had approved a new compilation; and Chief Justice Whitfield, T. C. Catchings, and William H. Hardy, a prominent and public-spirited Gulfport attorney, had been commissioned to put it together. As soon as the legislators reconvened at the beginning of January, 1906, the two houses allocated different portions of the draft code to different committees for consideration. On the fourth of the month—the same day that the lawyers in the Legislature met to begin organizing the new bar association—the Jackson *Clarion Ledger* printed an open letter from Whitfield calling on the legislators to appoint a single committee to consider the proposed new code in its entirety. He and the other two commissioners, he pointed out, could not possibly spare the time from their other concerns to meet with a large number of separate committees. But his request was not complied with. The different committees went ahead and reshaped the portions of the new code allotted to them in whatever manner seemed to them best, without consulting the commission and without any knowledge of what their colleagues on other committees were doing with other sections.[9] The result was a new code that was full of defects,

7. John Ray Skates, Jr., *A History of the Mississippi Supreme Court, 1817–1948* (Jackson: Mississippi Bar Foundation, 1973), pp. 48–49, 64–65, 101–104. Kirwan, pp. 118–19, 167–72.

8. *Miss. Laws* (1906), c. 137.

9. *Clarion Ledger*, January 4, 1906, p. 2, col. 1. R. H. Thompson, *Mississippi Codes* (Biloxi, 1926), pp. 28–29.

which may have been another reason why many Mississippi lawyers at that time felt a need to organize and to co-operate more closely with one another.

Yet one more very important motive was the same one that had caused the state's first bar association to be formed in 1821, a desire to maintain high professional and ethical standards. In 1912 the members of one of the association's committees remarked in their report: "Those of us who were present at the birth of our Association will remember that one of the principal objects, for the accomplishment of which it was formed, was to maintain the honor and dignity of the profession by the cultivation of legal ethics."[10]

The new code of 1906 authorized the incorporation of a state bar association "upon the application of any twenty-five or more attorneys of this state." It also stated that all attorneys practicing in the state might become members upon application, provided they were willing to comply with all of the rules and regulations; but it then went on to state that the association could "refuse to admit any attorney if it shall not deem him to be a reputable member of the bar."

The 1892 *Code* had contained, as its sole reference to a state bar association, a provision that "any regularly incorporated bar association of this state shall have power to institute and prosecute any attorney, before any court having jurisdiction, to disbar him for willful violation of his duties as an attorney or misconduct in his office."[11] The 1906 *Code* incorporated the same provision, but added to it two extra sections that went into much more detail as to requirements and procedures.[12] A state bar association would have for the future not only a right but also a "duty to receive, consider, and take action upon all complaints or charges which may be filed with or submitted to it . . . regarding the conduct of any attorney-at-law of this state, . . . alleged to be in violation of his professional duties." Furthermore, it was given the power to institute inquiries

10. Report of the Committee on the A.B.A. Code of Ethics, *Proc.* (1912), p. 22.

11. *Miss. Code* (1906), sec. 223. *Ibid.* (1892), sec. 223.

12. *Ibid.*, secs. 223, 223^a, 223^b, 223^d.

into cases of professional misconduct upon its own initiative. A committee was to be established to conduct such inquiries, and that committee would have full *subpoena* powers and the right to take testimony given on oath. The courts were authorized to give the committee any backing that it needed by use of the power to punish contempt of court, and all Mississippi attorneys were placed under an obligation to inform the committee of any wrongdoing by a colleague that came to their notice. Once the committee had delivered its written report to the association and the association had concluded that any "attorney of this state has been guilty of any violation of his duties as an attorney, or of misconduct in his office," then it was up to the association "to designate a committee which shall . . . prosecute him before any court having jurisdiction for the purpose of disbarring him." A bar association was even authorized, indeed obliged, to investigate complaints of wrongdoing by any of the state's judges and to report their findings to the Legislature.[13] Since none of these provisions is to be found in any of the state statutes passed between 1892 and 1906, they were presumably inserted directly into the expanded section 223 of the new code by those legislators who were active in founding the new bar association. And they indicate very clearly a determination to maintain high standards in face of whatever excesses the new radicalism in state politics might lead to.

The motion adopted at the meeting of lawyer-legislators on January 4, 1906, calling for an organized bar group, contained an additional provision that "all lawyers of the State of Mississippi are requested to meet in the House of Representatives . . . on the 25th day of January . . . for the purpose of forming a permanent State Bar Association." The newspapers were requested to advertise the meeting, and a motion, put forward by Representative E. E. Brown of Adams County, was passed calling on the chair to appoint an arrangements committee to make advance preparations. Besides Brown himself, Sydney Smith, Catchings, and Mixon were named to the committee along with Senator C. C. Dunn of Lauderdale

13. *Ibid.*, secs. 223[a], 223[b].

County, E. H. Moore of Bolivar County, president *pro tem* of the Senate, and Representative John G. Millsaps of Clay County.[14] The seven met the very next morning, Friday, January 5, and began making plans for the event, which was only three weeks away and which the *Clarion Ledger* had "no doubt" would be attended by "lawyers from all parts of the state." Hardin H. Brooks, it was decided, should once again start off the proceedings as temporary chairman. T. A. McWillie, who had served as president of the earlier bar association in 1892–93 and who, as senior surviving partner of the Jackson law firm Nugent and McWillie, enjoyed a "large and lucrative practice" in the capital city, would make the welcoming address; A. F. Fox of West Point, a former congressman and a 1903 gubernatorial candidate, would respond. Then Chief Justice Whitfield would be elected permanent chairman and deliver a keynote address explaining the reasons for holding the meeting.[15]

By the 24th of January everything was arranged; lawyers were arriving on every train that came into Jackson's railroad station all that afternoon and evening to take part in what the *Clarion Ledger* called the "reorganization of the Mississippi Bar Association." The meeting on the 25th, the newspaper noted, promised to be "a most important one" in which "several changes will be made in the existing rules of the organization."[16] It is interesting to note that the editor, and presumably others as well, apparently regarded what was happening as a revival of the moribund association originally founded in 1886 rather than the establishment of a totally new body.

Be that as it may, on Thursday the 25th "a large and enthusiastic meeting of attorneys at law," some 300 in number, gathered at 3:30 in the afternoon in the Hall of the House of Representatives in what the *Clarion Ledger* considered to be "perhaps the most distinguished gathering of attorneys in the recent history of the state." The plans made by the committee on the 5th had been altered to

---

14. *Proc.* (1906), p. 8.

15. *Clarion Ledger*, January 6, 1906, p. 8, col. 1. Dunbar Rowland, *Courts, Judges, and Lawyers of Mississippi, 1798–1935* (Jackson: State Department of Archives and History, 1935), pp. 240–41. *Early Mississippi Bar Associations*, p. 23.

16. January 25, 1906, p. 8, col. 1.

some extent. Hardin Brooks took the chair and opened the meeting, but it was C. H. Alexander, another noted Jackson attorney, rather than McWillie who made the welcoming speech on behalf of the Jackson bar; and Judge D. W. Houston of Aberdeen, rather than A. F. Fox, responded for the lawyers of the state. After their eloquence had been "heartily applauded," Chief Justice Whitfield was elected permanent chairman as planned, and W. W. Magruder of Starkville was chosen to serve as permanent secretary.

After the opening formalities were concluded, Whitfield explained the nature of the proposed organization and the intended scope of its work in an "eloquent and forcible speech" which drew "prolonged applause" from the audience. The next speaker was G. D. Shands, a former two-term lieutenant governor (1880–1888) who was now serving as Dean and Senior Professor of Law at the University of Mississippi at Oxford. He told those assembled that in his opinion a bar association was "urgently needed." Then his colleague, Thomas H. Somerville, the Junior Professor of Law at the University, originally from Winona, spoke also in favor of the association which he said was "greatly needed." State Senator Murray F. Smith from Vicksburg argued strongly "against letting the present loose system of legal practice in the state continue," and a concluding speech was made by E. F. Noel. After the speeches a nine-man committee was chosen and charged with drafting a constitution and by-laws for the new group; the committee included John Millsaps, E. H. Moore, C. C. Dunn, Sydney Smith, Attorney General Williams, E. E. Brown, C. L. Sivley, W. J. Lamb, and J. H. Neville. The meeting was then adjourned until eight o'clock that same evening.[17]

As the first item of business at the evening session, the constitution drafted by the committee of nine was formally approved (see appendix II). When that had been done, those present who qualified and wished to do so voted to resolve themselves into the "Mississippi State Bar Association." Altogether 207 lawyers enrolled. After their names had been taken, they proceeded to the

17. *Proc.* (1906), p. 9. *Clarion Ledger*, January 26, 1906, p. 5, cols. 1–2. Robert J. Farley, "The School of Law Since 1854," *Miss. LJ*, XX (1949), 250.

election of the officers required by article V of the new constitution: a president and three vice-presidents. When the balloting was concluded, G. D. Shands had been chosen as president and C. H. Alexander, D. W. Houston, and J. H. Neville as vice-presidents. In accordance with article VI a board of fifteen directors was next elected, five from each of the state's three Supreme Court districts. Those chosen were Murray F. Smith, E. F. Noel, C. C. Dunn, H. H. Brooks, John Millsaps, C. L. Sivley, W. W. Magruder, E. E. Brown, C. M. Williamson, W. J. East, Hugh K. Mahon, D. A. McIntosh, E. M. Barber, W. H. Hughes, and W. D. Bullard. And then again in accordance with article V, the newly elected directors met and chose Murray F. Smith to be their chairman and Sydney Smith to be the Association's first secretary-treasurer.

The next order of business was the giving of the members' approval to the set of by-laws also drafted by the committee of nine (see appendix II). When that had been done, on a motion by E. H. Moore, it was ordered that the president "obtain from the state of Mississippi a charter for the incorporation of this Association, when the Code of Laws adopted by the Legislature of 1906 becomes operative and effective." J. S. Sexton, a "progressive and able" lawyer from Hazlehurst, Murray F. Smith, Professor Somerville, and E. H. Moore were chosen as delegates to the next annual convention of the American Bar Association. E. F. Noel, W. B. Mixon, L. J. Farley, and G. J. Leftwich were picked as alternate delegates. The evening's proceedings ended with "quite a heated discussion" as to where the first annual meeting should be held the following June 19. C. H. Alexander urged the members to vote for a return to Jackson. J. H. Neville insisted strenuously that they ought to decide to go down to his hometown, Gulfport, instead. Neville was seconded by J. B. Errington of Hazlehurst, who argued that Gulfport with its many bars was the natural habitat of a Mississippi Bar Association. Gulfport was finally chosen, and "there being no further business the Association adjourned."[18]

---

18. *Proc.* (1906), pp. 10–19. Rowland, p. 234. *Clarion Ledger*, January 26, 1906, p. 5, cols. 1–2. That same day a Mississippi Sheriff's Association was also organized in Jackson with over fifty members, and the newspaper noted that Chief Justice Whitfield was not speaking to Attorney General Williams because of the Sandy Bayou controversy. *Ibid.*, January 26, 1906, p. 5, cols. 4–5.

It is not surprising that the members picked a site on the Gulf coast; "Mississippi's Riviera" not only had its bars, but also could boast of its sunshine, sea-air, seafood, and every kind of indoor and outdoor entertainment for the first annual meeting of the Association. Gulfport and Biloxi between them have hosted a majority of the meetings held during the seventy-plus years of the Association's history.

During the five-month interval between the organizational meeting and that first meeting, President Shands and Secretary-Treasurer Smith must have been extremely busy making preparations. The new state code was approved on April 21, considerably expanding the scope of the Association's authorized activities,[19] and six standing committees were quickly organized as follows:

JURISPRUDENCE AND LAW REFORM

T. A. McWillie, Jackson, Chairman

E. O. Sykes, Sr., Aberdeen	J. S. Sexton, Hazlehurst
Walter Sillers, Rosedale	L. F. Rainwater, Sardis

JUDICIAL ADMINISTRATION AND REMEDIAL PROCEDURE

J. H. Price, Magnolia, Chairman

J. C. Wilson, Oxford	J. Q. Robbins, Tupelo
H. C. Niles, Kosciusko	S. C. Cook, Clarksdale

LEGAL EDUCATION AND ADMISSION TO THE BAR

T. H. Somerville, University, Chairman

W. R. Harper, Jackson	Joseph Hirsh, Vicksburg
C. C. Dunn, Meridian	J. G. Millsaps, West Point

PUBLICATION

E. E. Brown, Natchez, Chairman

S. A. Morrison, Grenada	T. B. Dudley, Sumner
H. B. Greaves, Canton	H. H. Brooks, Jr., Macon

GRIEVANCES

C. H. Alexander, Jackson, Chairman

George J. Leftwich, Aberdeen	R. N. Miller, Hazlehurst
J. H. Neville, Gulfport	F. A. Montgomery, Tunica

OBITUARIES AND MEMORIALS

W. W. Magruder, Starkville, Chairman

Van B. Boddie, Greenville	H. K. Mahon, Holly Springs
A. T. Dent, Macon	W. D. Bullard, Pascagoula

---

19. *Miss. Laws* (1906), c. 101. The Code did not become operative until October, 1906. For some unknown reason the Association never did obtain a formal charter of incorporation from the Secretary of State's office.

The pattern for the committees undoubtedly was suggested by that of the American Bar Association which since 1881 had had standing committees with the same names as the first three and the last. It also no doubt derived to a very large extent from the earlier Mississippi Association founded in 1886 which had also had the same first three and a "Grievances" committee as well.[20]

By June 19 the committee members had already been working for some time on their respective assignments, and all was in readiness for the two-day annual meeting. Some 250 delegates showed up at Gulfport, and the *Clarion Ledger's* special reporter on the scene was sure that "a more intellectual body never assembled in convention in Mississippi." Supreme Court justices, chancellors and circuit court judges, district attorneys, and other members of the bar both young and old were in attendance. A full quorum of the state Senate had come and enough of the representatives that a special session of the Legislature could very easily have been arranged. Of the gubernatorial hopefuls in the coming primary elections, Jeff Truly (who had resigned from the Supreme Court to run), E. F. Noel, and Earl Brewer were present for the opening on the 19th, and Charles Scott and T. U. Sisson arrived on the 20th. Of the announced candidates apparently only E. N. Thomas failed to put in an appearance. Most of the delegates stayed at Gulfport's Great Southern Hotel. Others were guests of "Mine Host" McAlpine at the New Beach or stayed with local friends and used the Coast Traction Company's cars to get to and from the sessions.[21]

Just before noon on June 19 the members began leaving the lobbies of their respective hotels to converge on the Harrison County courthouse. There, at twelve o'clock, President Shands rapped his gavel in the courtroom and called the meeting to order. He faced a "cultured audience," made up not only of lawyers and their families but also of numerous Gulfport citizens who had come to enjoy the expected feast of oratory. In the first decade of the twen-

---

20. *Proc.* (1906), p. 6. The first committee is wrongly labelled "Jurisdiction and Law Reform." Friedman, p. 563. *Early Mississippi Bar Associations*, p. 21.

21. *Clarion Ledger*, June 20, 1906, p. 1, col. 4. McLemore, II, 41. Skates, p. 101.

tieth century, before radio, television, or even movies, listening to professional speechmakers was still a very popular American pastime, and the audience was not to be disappointed. After the opening prayer of invocation had been offered by the Reverend G. H. Galloway, a local minister, the Honorable E. J. Bowers, a Bay St. Louis lawyer who represented that district in the United States Congress, was introduced to make the welcoming address. Gulfport, which was rapidly developing into one of America's major convention cities, he observed, had never been more honored than it was that day, for all Mississippians were "proud of the bench and bar of Mississippi." Theirs was a grave responsibility, he told the Association's members: "Whatever of reform there is needed in the practice of our great and noble profession, whatever of reform is needed in the laws of the state, whatever of judicial reform, if any is needed, it becomes your duty to point it out and to give the impetus of your great weight and influence to its accomplishment." Finally, wishing them "God Speed" in their labors, he again assured them of Gulfport's welcome.[22]

President Shands thanked Congressman Bowers for his remarks. Then Vice-President Alexander, amidst applause, took the chair while Shands himself advanced to the podium to give his annual address. Although article XIII of the Constitution called for the president to open each annual meeting with "an address, in which he shall communicate the most noteworthy changes in the statute law, on points of general interest, made in the state and by the Congress during the preceding year," Shands pleaded that in his brief tenure of office he had not had sufficient time to study the latest enactments of either Congress or the state Legislature. Instead, he chose to talk "on matters of general interest to the Association." Unfortunately no complete record was kept of what he said, but his speech left his listeners, according to the *Clarion Ledger*, in no doubt that they were hearing "one of the best speakers in the state." His words were so "well chosen and masterfully

22. Accounts of the speeches and other business of the meeting are taken from the *Clarion Ledger*, June 20, 1906, p. 1, col. 4 and June 21, 1906, p. 1, col. 4, and from *Proc.* (1906), pp. 20–57.

delivered" that "every period was rounded out with applause and cheers." His "love for his noble profession and his co-workers was apparent," and "at times his enthusiasm could not be bridled" with the result that "while he intended to utter only what was written on the paper he at times branched out or enlarged on his notes." His speech throughout was "filled with suggestions which the association," the newspaper's representative thought, "would do well to adopt."

The only other featured speaker on the two-day program was sixth district chancellor James F. McCool of Kosciusko, who spoke at the evening session on the 19th. He had some serious suggestions to make: that stenographers should be hired to keep records of trials in the chancery courts and that chancellors' and circuit judges' salaries should be raised to the point where it was no longer possible for their court clerks to earn twice as much in a year as they did. But, as suited the lateness of the hour, his speech was primarily a humorous one, being frequently "interrupted by applause and laughter."

Besides listening to speeches there was business to be done. Secretary-Treasurer Smith's report showed that 163 lawyers had paid their annual membership dues of five dollars—still the same amount that one had had to pay to belong to the first state bar association founded in 1821—at the January 25 organizational meeting. Since then forty-three more had paid up and been admitted, so that the 207 memberships pledged at Jackson had been just about achieved. On a motion by Murray F. Smith, it was voted that honorary membership, which exempted one from payment of dues, should be limited to those categories of persons specifically mentioned in the relevant article, number XVII, of the by-laws: all judges of the state's supreme, chancery, and circuit courts and the United States judge for the two Mississippi districts.

Besides the secretary-treasurer three of the six standing committees appointed by President Shands also had reports ready for presentation. T. A. McWillie, reporting for the Committee on Jurisprudence and Law Reform, said that, while its members generally favored a conservative approach to legal innovations, they did support "the endeavor to secure upon certain subjects of legislation uniformity in the laws of the several states as shown by the proceedings of the National Conference of Commissioners on Uniform State Laws" and believed that the Association should take steps to become involved in future sessions of that conference. They also had a specific recommendation to make concerning the state Supreme Court. They believed that the number of justices ought to be increased by constitutional amendment from three to five. The Committee on Judicial Administration and Remedial Procedure, in their report presented by J. H. Price of Magnolia, concurred in the need for an increased number of Supreme Court justices. However, they suggested that the Association might wish to consider recommending that the number be raised to six and that the court then be divided into two sections of three justices each, one for civil and one for criminal appeals. Professor Somerville gave the report from the Committee on Legal Education and Admission to the Bar at the final session on the morning of June 20th. Its members were all of the opinion that five additional areas of law ought to be covered in future bar exams: corporations, partnerships, torts, insurance, and private international law. And they urged the Association to strive from the outset "to create and maintain a strong and healthy sentiment in favor of high standards both as to knowledge of the law and the ethics of the profession." Finally, since under the new code responsibility for bar admissions was to be transferred away from the overburdened Supreme Court justices to the chancellors, they hoped that members would "do all in their power to assist the chancellors in discharge of the duties confided to them touching this subject."

Recommendations made in the speeches and in the committee reports were reflected in the resolutions passed by those attending the meeting. The hiring of stenographers for the chancery courts was endorsed. The president was called upon to appoint a committee of three who would establish a connection with the Uniform State Laws Commissioners and attend their next annual meeting. He was also required, upon a motion made by W. Calvin Wells, Jr. of Jackson, to approve a second three-man committee to draft an amendment to the constitution for "at least five Judges of the Supreme Court; one to be appointed for and from each Supreme Court district, and the remainder from the State at large." This committee was also to draft a proposed statute which would create two "Supreme Court Commissioners, whose duty it shall be to sit with the Judges of the Supreme Court . . . and consult with and assist them in all proper ways," but without power to vote as to how cases should be decided. The commissioners, it was considered, could take some of the load off of the shoulders of the justices of the highest court while the constitutional amendment to increase their number was going through the lengthy process of adoption. Once it had drafted the proposed amendment and statute, the committee was then to lobby the members of the Legislature for their adoption.

With regard to their own internal affairs, the Association resolved that their president should set up yet another *ad hoc* committee, consisting of S. M. Smith, Alexander, Catchings, Shands, and Somerville, to draft a proposed code of ethics for presentation at the next annual meeting. It was resolved also that the directors should be reimbursed out of Association funds for all travel and other expenses incurred in the performance of their duties except for attendance at annual meetings. With regard to annual meetings, the directors were requested to fix upon a set time each year for the Association to meet and to urge the Legislature to so arrange the terms of the chancery and circuit courts that there would be no conflicts.[23] Meanwhile, it was decided to accept an invitation extended by the Vicksburg bar to meet in that city in 1907, beginning at twelve noon on the second Tuesday in May. It was further decided that a formal banquet should be a feature of all future meetings, with the Association paying the bill provided that the cost did not exceed half the total amount then in the treasury.

The major business at the final session on the morning of the 20th was the election of officers for the coming year. In fact very

---

23. Farley, p. 250. Dunbar Rowland, *Mississippi* (3 vols.; Atlanta: Southern Historical Publishing Association, 1907), III, 752–53.

few changes were made in the slate elected the previous January. Shands, who would soon be leaving the state to occupy a chair of law at Tulane University, was replaced as president by Murray F. Smith, who had been practicing law in Vicksburg since 1874 when he arrived there from his native North Carolina. A member of the state constitutional convention in 1890, he had long represented Warren and Hinds counties in the upper house of the Legislature. Alexander, Houston, and Neville were re-elected as vice-presidents. Leroy Percy of Greenville replaced M. F. Smith on the board of directors, which otherwise remained unchanged. And the directors, after electing C. L. Sivley as their new chairman, re-elected S. M. Smith as the Association's secretary-treasurer.

At 3:00 P.M. on the afternoon of the 20th, their business accomplished, those Association members and their families who had not yet set off on their journeys home enjoyed a boating excursion on the Gulf as guests of the Progressive Business League of Gulfport. They travelled aboard the *Rambler*, "one of the finest launches in the South," and their hosts proudly showed them the work that had already been accomplished in dredging out a "magnificent channel" whereby ocean-going vessels from every corner of the globe could carry goods into and out of Mississippi. After almost five decades of civil war, political strife, and economic stagnation, the state was at last ready to play a major part once more as an economic, political, and cultural force in the United States and in the world. To her lawyers would fall the task of providing assistance and advice to her government leaders, her businessmen, and her citizens in every walk of life, help that would come to be ever more urgently needed as modern life became steadily more complex. It would be up to the organized state bar, by raising the standards of legal practice and widening the horizons of legal knowledge, to see that they performed that task in a manner that ensured to every Mississippian a better life under the law in the twentieth century.

II

The Early Years of the Bar Association

1907–1918

DURING THE FIRST dozen years of its corporate existence, Mississippi's new State Bar Association continued along comfortably enough, achieving few major successes but at the same time suffering no really serious setbacks. It reflected in fact the history of the state itself down to 1914. In spite of the arrival of the boll weevil on the cotton plantations, the Mississippi economy continued to grow slowly and the people enjoyed a slowly improving standard of living. Then, in August, 1914, World War I began in Europe. In April, 1917, as a result of the sinking by a German submarine of the British liner *Lusitania* with many American passengers on board, the United States entered the war. Mississippi's agricultural products increased in demand and rose rapidly in price. The state's economy boomed, and at the same time the old ways began to be subjected to external forces of change which affected the life of every Mississippian, including of course the members of the Bar Association.

Association membership—not including the federal and state judges who were entitled to be honorary members—in 1909 reached a peak of 330 out of a total bar enrollment of 1026. But in the following decade, even though the number of lawyers in the state increased by nearly thirty percent to just under 1300, the Association's membership stabilized at around 260, about twenty percent of the total possible.[1] Undoubtedly the most outstanding and active member during the period was Sydney Smith, who con-

1. *Proc.* (1909), pp. 24–28, 124–38. *Procs.* (1910–1918), *passim.*

tinued to be re-elected secretary-treasurer until the annual meeting of 1914 when he was chosen president for the ensuing year. Commissioned as circuit judge for the fourth district about the same time that he first became secretary in 1906, Smith, in 1909, was appointed to the state Supreme Court by his fellow Holmescountian, Governor Edmund F. Noel; and in 1912, on the resignation of Robert B. Mayes from that post, he became chief justice. He was still presiding over the court when he died at the age of seventy-nine thirty-six years later in 1948, thereby setting the record both for the longest term served on the court and for the longest term as chief justice.[2] For the first eight years of its history, therefore, the Association had a judge serving as its secretary, and from 1912 to 1914 it had the chief justice. It was Mayes whom Smith succeeded as president in 1914, just as two years before he had succeeded him as chief justice. State Senator James R. McDowell of Jackson, a pioneer champion of child labor laws in the state, was chosen in 1914 to replace Smith as secretary-treasurer and was re-elected each year through 1917 when he resigned the position to go into the army.[3]

No doubt in order to arouse widespread interest among Mississippi lawyers and thereby to attract members and encourage attendance, the annual meetings during this period were held in different cities around the central area of the state. Only Vicksburg, in 1907 and 1915, and Jackson, in 1912 and 1918, were visited twice; and the state capital was selected as the meeting place in 1912 only after Greenville, the intended site, had been hit by a severe flood. Other cities visited were Meridian (1908), West Point (1909), Natchez (1910), Hattiesburg (1911), Greenwood (1913), Laurel (1916), and Greenville (1917). In 1914 the Association returned once more to Gulfport, the site of its first annual gathering, for a joint meeting with the Louisiana State Bar. Some 160 members registered for the Gulfport meeting, but the usual attendance each year was between 120 and 150, or about fifty percent of the

2. Skates, p. 95.
3. *Procs.*, *passim.* McLemore, II, 46.

total membership.[4] From 1907 to 1913 the meetings were always three-day affairs, beginning the Tuesday after the first Monday in May and running through Thursday. Perhaps in order to cut costs and thus again to encourage more members to attend, beginning with the Gulfport meeting in 1914 the program was limited to the two days that it had been in 1906.

For those members who could afford the time and the money and were willing to take the trouble to attend them, the annual meetings of the Association provided a valuable opportunity for stimulating encounters with attorneys from other areas of Mississippi and for catching up on the latest developments in the law at both the state and national levels. That was important at a time when the train was still the only means of fast, long distance travel, and most lawyers otherwise would go from one end of a year to the next without ever meeting any colleagues who were not from the same town or county, or at least from the same judicial circuit or chancery district. The meetings also provided the opportunity for a brief vacation spent in one of the state's larger and more interesting towns. Not surprisingly their wives, and sometimes other family members as well, accompanied bar members in order to have a little holiday also. In 1908 it was resolved that, because their presence would "lend grace and dignity to its annual meeting and wisdom of [*sic*] its deliberations," members in the future were "invited to attend sessions accompanied by their wives, daughters, sisters, and sweethearts as the condition may then exist." In accordance with the resolution passed in 1906, the first annual banquet was held in 1907, and for the next four years after that it was always scheduled for the last night of the meeting. But there were invariably some members who wanted to hurry home immediately, and so in 1911 it was resolved to leave it to the discretion of the directors when to hold the banquet each year. In 1917, on a motion by Leroy Percy, seconded by W. H. Powell of Canton, ladies were for the first time invited to attend the banquet.

4. *Procs.* (1910–1918), *passim.* About ten percent of the lawyers in the state attended, approximately the same percentage that attends in the 1970's.

One may presume that their presence thereafter resulted in a certain refining of the tone of the afterdinner toasts and speeches.

The passage of the state statute which became law on December 31, 1908,[5] outlawing the selling or serving of beers, wines, or spirits, was a long time in having any effect on the Bar Association's banquet menus. In 1909 the menu offered on May 7 by the Hotel Holt in West Point included "Manhattan Cocktail, Burgundy Splits," and "Mumm's Extra Dry." Even as late as 1912, in Jackson, the state capital, the banquet menu at the Edwards Hotel offered Liebfraumilch to go with the soft shell crabs and sauce tartare, and Mumm's Extra Dry champagne (evidently a favorite with the bar) to accompany the main course of broiled squabs with new potatoes au parmesan and green peas. Not until 1913 at Reiman's Hotel in Greenwood was a banquet menu offered that for the first time included no alcoholic beverages. But then the following year, at Gulfport for the joint-meeting with the Louisiana Bar Association, at the banquet held at the Grand Southern Hotel, things were again done, as one would expect, very much *comme il faut*. Martini cocktails accompanied the oysters on the half shell. The turtle soup was Madeira-flavored, and *Vino de Pasto* was served with the sheephead in white wine sauce. For the main dish one could have burgundy with the *Medaillon de Boeuf* and *Richelieu* or dry sauterne with the *Capon Eglantine*. Roederer *Grand Vin Sec* was available with the savory pigeon, dessert, cheese and biscuits; and finally there was cognac to go with the *cafe noir*, cigars, and cigarettes. After that no more alcoholic beverages, however. At Vicksburg in 1915 no wines or spirits were listed on the banquet menu offered by the National Park Hotel. At Laurel in 1916 the Hotel Pinehurst offered "Punch au Rhum" between the main course and the dessert, but presumably it was made up of fruit juices with artificial rum flavoring.

Though they might connive at breaches of the state's liquor laws, the Bar Association at the same time was determined to establish and enforce a high standard of professional conduct. At Vicks-

5. *Miss. Laws* (1908), c. 113.

burg, on May 8, 1907, the members adopted the code of ethics that had been drafted for them by the committee appointed for that purpose the year before at Gulfport. The preamble attached to the Code voiced their recognition of the fact that "the purity and efficiency of judicial administration" depended just "as much upon the character, conduct, and demeanor of attorneys in this great trust, as upon fidelity and learning of courts [*sic*], or the honesty and intelligence of juries." (See appendix III.) Two years later at West Point, in order that the majority of the state's lawyers who were not Association members and the general public would be better informed as to the ethical standards that were expected to be upheld, the members resolved to try to persuade the Legislature to publish the code as an appendix to the published report of the laws passed at its next session. The lawmakers, however, in session in 1910 declined to co-operate.

Meanwhile, at the 1908 meeting in Meridian, a resolution had passed calling on President James S. Sexton to appoint a committee of three to work with the American Bar Association committee which was at that time already engaged in drafting a code of ethics for the national body. Sexton chose for the job Professor Somerville, who had played a leading role in drafting the Mississippi ethical code, Tim E. Cooper of Jackson, and S. A. Witherspoon, Jr. of Meridian. However, of the three appointed, only Witherspoon was present in Seattle together with Sexton and Adam T. Stovall of Okolona, when, three months later on August 27, 1908, the thirty-first annual meeting of the A.B.A. adopted its thirty-two article "Canon of Professional Ethics."[6] Three years later, at Hattiesburg in 1911, the members of the Mississippi Association appointed T. A. McWillie, Sydney Smith, and W. D. Anderson of Tupelo as a committee to consider and report on whether the A.B.A. code should be adopted for the state.

At the 1912 meeting in Jackson, a momentous one that saw

---

6. *Procs.* (1923), pp. 91–92. A.B.A., *Annual Report* (1908), *passim.* Presumably Somerville and Cooper had communicated their ideas on the A.B.A. Code to Witherspoon.

many changes made in the Association's structure and rules, the committee made its report. The A.B.A. code, it had decided, was "a great improvement on the one now governing our Association." They recalled that the drafters of the A.B.A. document had hoped when they drew it up that it would eventually be adopted by every state bar association, and they themselves were convinced that having a uniform canon of professional ethics in force throughout the entire nation was highly desirable. In fact they were prepared to go so far as to say that "in our judgment, the adoption of this Code of Ethics is not only advisable, but is imperatively necessary, if this Association is to do its full part in maintaining the honor and dignity of the profession." The members were persuaded and the committee's report adopted. The thirty-two articles of the A.B.A. code thus became the standard for Mississippi lawyers also. Two other recommendations made by the committee were also based on recommendations made by the A.B.A. in 1908; that all law schools in the state should include a course in legal ethics in their curriculum and that all candidates for admission to the bar should be examined on them. These were adopted by the Association at the same time.[7]

Besides adopting the A.B.A. code of ethics, the members at this 1912 meeting also made some major changes in the constitution and by-laws that had been adopted at the organizational meeting of the Association in Jackson on January 25, 1906. Four years earlier, in 1908, article III of the constitution, dealing with the admission of new members, had been reworded to require that each applicant for membership have his application endorsed by two lawyers who were already members before submitting it to the Board of Directors. Presumably the change was intended to save the directors from the embarrassment of having to reject an application. Nowhere in any of the *Proceedings* is there any mention of a membership application being turned down or even put to a

7. Edson R. Sunderland, *History of the American Bar Association And Its Work* (Ann Arbor 1953), pp. 111–112.

ballot; so whatever screening out of undesirables occurred must have been done by the Board. In 1907 the first change in the by-laws had been made. The directors had been asked the year before to fix a set day for the meetings to begin each year, and at their suggestion a nineteenth article was added making the first Tuesday after the first Monday in May the opening day for the future. However, in 1912 the meeting in Jackson did not begin until Wednesday, May 8, because of the presidential primary held in the state the previous day.

The main change made in the Association's organizational structure at that 1912 meeting was the elimination of the Board of Directors. It must always have been difficult during the preceding six years to arrange a time when even a bare majority of fifteen busy professional men could be brought together for a meeting. And the cost of their travel expenses from all over the state to wherever the meeting was held (usually Jackson or the president's hometown) must have put a strain on the Association's limited budget. Those must have been the main reasons why article V of the constitution was rewritten in part in 1912 so as to state: "The Officers of this Association shall consist of one President, one Vice-President, a Secretary and Treasurer, and an Executive Committee. . . ." A further change provided for the secretary-treasurer to be elected in the future by the Executive Committee, which, according to a revised article VI, was to

> consist of five members, consisting of the President, who shall be *ex officio* chairman thereof, the Vice-President, and one member to be elected from each Supreme Court District as now constituted, and shall discharge such duties as shall be imposed upon it by the By-Laws. It may be called together by the President, or by any three members thereof.

Several lesser changes were also made. Article III was rewritten so as to transfer to the new Executive Committee responsibility for screening membership applications. Article XI, which dealt with the other duties of the Board of Directors, was totally deleted, and article XIII was changed to include a provision that the vice-president should succeed to the office of president if it ever became vacant "by death, resignation or otherwise."[8]

In addition, the by-laws were amended, substituting "Executive Committee" for "Board of Directors" wherever necessary. And Section II of the by-laws was changed to require the secretary-treasurer to be bonded in the amount of two thousand, rather than one thousand, dollars. It was a step that was long overdue, although the Association's budget in 1906 had involved only $1,030. In 1911–12, $1,161.29 had been spent, and the balance on hand as of April 5, 1912, according to Sydney Smith's report, was $2,313.14. At this period in the Association's history the largest single expenditure each year was for the annual banquet, which at Hattiesburg in 1911 had cost $372.04. The next largest cost was that of printing the annual *Proceedings* for which Hederman Brothers had been paid $301.25 in 1911. And then there was the secretary-treasurer's salary of $300 which was paid in two installments of $150 each, one in November and one in May. Other disbursements were of only a few dollars, sometimes just a few cents, for such items as stationery, stamps, telephone calls, and travel expenses.

One item in the 1911 budget was $22 for the "annual orator," and the amended article III of the by-laws in 1912 ordered the newly-constituted executive committee each year to "select some person to make an address at [the] annual meeting." In fact, back in 1909, at the meeting held in the Masonic Hall at West Point, the members had first enjoyed what was to become a regular feature of the annual meetings for the next several decades, the delivery of the "annual address" by a distinguished member of the bar from outside the state. On that occasion the honored visitor was E. T. Merrick, a New Orleans lawyer, who spoke on "The Tendency of Modern Legislation in the South," deploring the in-

---

8. Happily no president of the association has ever died while in office, but in 1913, the very next year, President R. N. Miller was unable to attend because of the recent death of his wife. Vice-President A. W. Shands, therefore, presided in his stead, and, when Shands was called away by an emergency on the third day of the meeting, E. F. Noel was elected "president pro-tem."

hibiting effect on interstate commerce of regulatory business legislation enacted by smallminded state legislators. "Either," he concluded prophetically, "there must come a new written Constitution, or the slow evolution of an unwritten Constitution by which State lines will either be eliminated or modified so as to leave this great Union one homogeneous land."

Although Association members generally favored a uniform system of commercial laws, pleas for stronger federal controls would rarely be heard at their meetings. Much more typical were the sentiments expressed in the second annual address, delivered at Natchez in 1910 by Wilson E. Hemingway of Little Rock, Arkansas, who lamented "the growth of national influence under the power to regulate interstate commerce." The railroads were, of course, the principal arteries of Mississippi's commerce at that time. In 1913 Blewett Lee, a native Mississippian working in Chicago as a lawyer for the railroads, in an annual address on "Anti-Railroad Personal Injury Litigation" pleaded for a fairer deal for his clients from Mississippi juries and judges. And in 1916 T. Marshall Miller of New Orleans, speaking on "The Railroads and the People," appealed for a better understanding by customers of the reasons behind railroad freight-rate and fare setting policies. By the time the Association met again in May, 1917, the United States had become involved on the side of the allies in World War I; thus it was appropriate that Governor Charles H. Brough of Arkansas chose as his topic "Southern Jurisprudence and American Patriotism." And in 1918 Assistant United States Attorney General W. C. Fitts, visiting from Washington, expounded on America's legitimate grievance in international law against Germany over the sinking of the *Lusitania.*

The Association's various presidents during this period generally obeyed the injunction in article XIII of the constitution that they should open each annual meeting by giving a report on "the most noteworthy changes" in state and federal legislation during the preceding year. But C. H. Alexander in 1908 chose instead to speak on "How the States Have Fared During the Last Decade in the Supreme Court of the United States." As he saw it, it had been the Court, rather than Congress or the executive branch, that had been "the strong bulwark for the protection of the rights of States against Federal Encroachment." And he was optimistic that in the long run the American citizen, and especially the worker, would come to realize "that the State not the Federal government, is his best guardian and protector." In 1915 Sydney Smith chose to devote all of his speech to a plea for the reforms that he wanted to see made in Mississippi's court system.[9] And in 1917, A. T. Stovall, before he reported on recent legislation, availed himself of the opportunity to advocate certain changes he felt were needed in the state's "terribly outdated" jury selection methods.[10]

Looking at the various speeches made or papers read during the period by rank and file members of the Association, one finds that the desirability of a uniform system of commercial legislation throughout all of the states was the subject most frequently treated. Railroad-connected legal problems again were a favorite topic and so were problems connected with appeal procedures in the state courts. As one would expect, there were also a good many discussions of the various problems faced by the lawyer in his everyday practice. Finally, reminiscences of great lawyers in Mississippi's past, or of what it was like to practice law in the state several decades back, given by some of the grand old men of the bar were often frequent items on the programs.

However, the members were not limited to lawyers' matters and legal concerns. Other matters that affected life in the state also received their attention. A state in which yellow fever and malaria were still serious concerns and where pellagra and hookworm were endemic could not help being concerned with public health.[11] At their 1910 meeting a resolution was passed expressing support for a bill, then before the United States Senate, sponsored by Senator Owen of Oklahoma, to establish a national department of health.[12] Expanding industry and building up the white population were

9. See p. 36 herein.
10. See p. 32 herein.
11. McLemore, II, chap. 43 *passim.*
12. In 1912 the old U.S. Public Health and Marine Hospitals Service was reorganized as the "Public Health Service" under the Treasury Department. In 1953 it was incorporated into the new Department of Health, Education, and Welfare.

other items considered important, and in 1910 the Association also resolved that "strong and concerted efforts should be made to attract to this State desirable immigrants and . . . we heartily approve and endorse the State-wide Immigration Convention to be held June 21st and 22nd . . . in Jackson." Probably moved by a report published in 1916 by Whitman Davis, president of the Mississippi Library Association, which deplored the fact that only some twenty municipalities in the state had public libraries and which pointed out that "it is almost criminal for a state to teach the child to read and then not provide good books for him to read," the members in 1917 passed a resolution calling upon the Legislature at its next session to pass a county free library law.[13]

Members of a bar association, of course, were particularly interested in reading law books and law journals; however, very little of that nature was being published in Mississippi, and, although one of the six standing committees listed in article X of the constitution adopted in 1906 was a Publications Committee, it was inactive. Perhaps its members assisted the secretary-treasurer in getting out the *Proceedings* each year, but if so that was all they did. Then at the remarkable 1912 meeting in Jackson, at which so many innovations and changes were made, the committee was apparently circumvented—it was certainly disregarded—by the passage of a resolution moved by R. N. Miller of Hazlehurst which called on the president to appoint a board of five "directors" who were to establish as soon as possible, in the name of the Association, "a Magazine to be devoted to the interests of this association and to the lawyers of Mississippi. . . ." The resolution empowered the directors to arrange for the magazine's publication on a monthly schedule in Jackson. They were authorized to hire an editor-in-chief, and the heads of the state's two law schools, at the University and at Millsaps College, were to be asked to serve as associate or contributing editors.[14] The directors were to retain in their own

13. McLemore, II, 500. No such law was passed, and not until after World War II would Mississippi be provided with an adequate system of public libraries.

14. The law school at Millsaps, founded in 1896, lasted until 1918 when it ceased operating because the bulk of its students had joined the armed forces. See McLemore, II, 381.

hands control of general policy and the setting of subscription rates and advertising fees. Every member of the Association was urged to subscribe himself and to encourage other lawyers to do so. In order to get the magazine launched $1,000 of the Association's funds was set aside to cover its initial expenses, with the proviso that no more would be forthcoming and that publication must cease if that entire sum were ever spent. It was left to the directors' discretion, in fact, as to whether publication of such a magazine was feasible or not.

At the first business session in Greenwood the following year (1913), the five directors, R. H. Thompson, George W. May, George S. Butler, J. S. Sexton, and George J. Leftwich, reported their gloomy conclusions.[15] They had calculated that to be successful a magazine of the type called for would have to have at least 500 subscribers, each willing to pay a subscription of three dollars per year. A survey taken of the membership, however, had indicated that only 218 members were willing to pledge themselves to take out such a subscription. Income from advertisements in a magazine with such a limited readership, they had discovered, would be almost negligible. Therefore, though they had spent less than one hundred of the one thousand dollars allotted, it was their recommendation that the project be dropped. Some members were not easily discouraged, however, and a new committee, chaired by William Whittington of Greenwood, was appointed to review the directors' findings. But at the closing session two days later Whittington and his colleagues, W. A. Ellis of Carthage, Monroe McLurg of Greenwood, and S. D. Neill of Indianola, told the group that they concurred with what the directors had advised.[16] Evidently the time for a *Mississippi Law Journal* had not yet come.

In 1916 at Laurel, article X of the constitution was rewritten deleting the Committee on Publications and adding two new com-

15. None of these directors was on the "Publications Committee" for 1912–13.

16. Whittington's committee also recommended rejection of a proposal, made by R. H. Thompson, and referred to them, that the Association pay a year's subscription of $2 for each member to the *Southern Bench and Bar Review* which Charles George of San Francisco, publisher of the *Lawyer and Banker*, had recently begun publishing in Jackson. The Association concurred with their negative recommendation.

mittees: one on Professional Ethics and one on Legislation. There had been an *ad hoc* committee on professional ethics in existence since 1913, the same year in which the A.B.A. created a new standing committee with that name. Although in 1916 the state committee's chairman reported that only one ethical problem had ever been referred to it, and that had been in the first year of its existence, the Association's members evidently felt that making it a permanent standing committee would emphasize their dedication to ethical principles. As for the Committee on Legislation, it reflected the members' concern that so few of the measures that their group had advocated over the years had ever been enacted into law by the Legislature.

Five years earlier, in 1911, at Hattiesburg the Standing Committee on Jurisprudence and Law Reform had summarized for the members the legislative achievements gained by the Association in its first five years. Four of the measures that they had advocated had been enacted into law, all of them in the legislative session of 1910: an act creating Supreme Court Commissioners (c. 164), an act creating the office of county prosecuting attorney (c. 112), an act giving appellants an automatic right to receive the court stenographer's notes of the original trial (c. 111), and an act increasing the number of chancery and circuit court districts (cc. 104–05).

But six of the measures they had called for had not been enacted: one that would have authorized the governor to appoint three commissioners to represent the state at the meetings of the National Association for the Uniformity of Legislation in the Several States, one calling for a constitutional amendment to increase the number of state Supreme Court justices to five, one calling for a constitutional amendment to allow the state to be granted a change of *venire* in criminal cases on the same grounds as a defendant, one for an act ending the automatic right to an appeal from a conviction for a misdemeanor, one for an act whereby no judgment could be reversed for certain types of errors unless the record affirmatively showed that specific objection to those errors had been made and brought to the attention of the judge in the trial, and finally one recommending that common law forms of indictment be abolished as far as was possible while still preserving the accused's constitutional right to be fully informed of the nature of the accusation against him. A score of four out of ten was not bad in light of the Association's later record in prevailing upon the Legislature to pass the laws it wished for. But at this early stage in the group's history the members found it hard to understand why a legislative body which included so many of their fellow lawyers so rarely agreed with them as to what measures were desirable.

However, the members of the Bar Association themselves could not always agree on what should be done by way of reforms. At the 1912 meeting in Jackson the majority of those present voted to rescind the 1911 recommendation tightening up procedure in appeals for errors and also the one favoring the abolition of the old common law formulas for indictments, while at the same time reaffirming their support for a constitutional amendment giving the state the same right to ask for a change of *venire* in criminal cases that the defendant enjoyed. The 1912 meeting also voted in favor of the creation of an intermediate appellate court for the state which would have jurisdiction in civil cases involving a principal of $2,000 or less and in all misdemeanor cases, with the Supreme Court given the power to review the appellate court's decision by *certiorari* if it chose to do so. And, with regard to the Supreme Court itself, the members in 1912 voted their support for the idea, suggested in 1906 at Gulfport by the Committee on Judicial Administration and Remedial Procedure, of expanding the court to include six justices who would be authorized to sit in two divisions of three justices each operating by rules of the court's own devising.[17]

As for the legislators elected to the House and Senate in 1911, they seem to have been in favor of reforms, but also to have been very democratically inclined and not often willing to accept dictation from the rather *élite* group in the State Bar Association. In their 1912 session they made the new office of county prosecutor optional, with the people of each county voting on whether to have

---

17. See p. 17 herein.

such an offiicial on their payroll or not. They also inserted into the constitution an amendment making chancery and circuit judgeships elective. As for the Supreme Court, the 1912 session repealed the 1910 statute authorizing the employment of two commissioners and left the court exactly as it had been when the Bar Association first recommended its expansion in 1906. However, in the 1914 session another constitutional amendment was proposed which would, as the Association had suggested two years earlier, expand the court to six justices sitting in two divisions and setting their own rules, but at the same time would make the justiceships elective and reduce the justices' terms of office from nine years to eight.[18]

Former Supreme Court Chief Justice Robert B. Mayes was one of those far from satisfied with such partial victories. In his presidential address to the Association's 1914 meeting at Gulfport—read by Vice-President George Leftwich because Mayes was absent due to ill health—he echoed the disappointment and pessimism of the 1911 committee report. The Bar Association, he asserted, could claim to have "done little else than cultivate social relations between its members, and has not obtained many improvements in the law or the mode of its administration." In spite of a great deal of hard work by committees and by individual members, "it has for some reason been unable to get the Legislature to adopt any of its recommendations." The solution, he felt, was to get every lawyer in the state into the Association in order that they all might "learn to know and appreciate what [it] is trying to accomplish." Mayes, who was to die in 1921, would not live long enough to see the unified bar come into being in 1932, nor to see that even an association to which all of the state's lawyers belonged could still have difficulty with the Legislature.

Some of the changes and reforms championed by the Association's members came out of their own personal experiences in their law offices and in the courts. But undoubtedly their major source of inspiration and ideas was the American Bar Association through

18. McLemore, II, 57–58. Skates, pp. 50–91. Another constitutional amendment enacted in 1914–16 reduced to nine the number of jurors required for a verdict in a civil trial.

its annual meetings and publications. During the decade 1908 to 1918 an average of six Mississippi Association members attended the A.B.A. meetings held each year in late August or early September, although those who went were by no means always the three delegates and three alternates formally chosen at the Association's annual meeting four months before. Some Mississippians, such as Congressman John M. Allen of Tupelo, S. A. Witherspoon of Meridian, B. E. Eaton of Gulfport, A. W. Shands of Sardis, A. T. Stovall of Okolona, and J. S. Sexton of Hazlehurst, went nearly every year. Others attended only once or twice. The location of the meeting to some extent, of course, affected the size of the attendance. Eleven Mississippi lawyers made the comparatively short trip to Chattanooga in 1910, and ten travelled on the Illinois Central up to Chicago in 1916. But as has been noted above, only Stovall and Witherspoon went all the way to Seattle in 1908, and Eaton and Shands were the only members to travel to Salt Lake City in 1915. In 1917, perhaps partly because of the war, Stovall was the only Mississippi representative present when the A.B.A. met again, for the first time in fifteen years, at its original home, Saratoga Springs, New York. But the distance to be travelled was not the only factor that affected attendance. The tourist appeal of the host city also made a difference. The largest delegation (twelve in number) went all the way up to Montreal, Canada, for the meeting there in 1913, and in 1911 as many as seven considered it worth their while to make the long trip to Boston.[19] In 1916, at Chicago, on the initiative of the then president of the A.B.A., Elihu Root of New York, a conference of local bar association delegates was held prior to the commencement of the main meeting to discuss ways of forming closer ties between the national association and state and local associations of lawyers. The conference was such a success that it was decided to make it a regular feature of A.B.A. meetings in the future. One of its recommendations, approved by the full A.B.A. meeting that same year, was that the president of each state bar association should become, *ex officio*, a

19. A.B.A., *Annual Report* (1908–1918), *passim*.

member of the A.B.A. General Council, provided he was an A.B.A. member and that the secretary of each state association, with the same provision, should become an *ex officio* member of the A.B.A. Local Council for the state.[20] At its 1917 meeting in Hattiesburg the Mississippi Association voted its endorsement of the new and closer relationship with the national body.

Four years earlier, at the 1913 meeting in Greenwood, the Mississippi Bar had passed a motion "heartily" endorsing the resolution passed by the A.B.A. in 1912 in Milwaukee "that a complete and uniform system of law pleading should prevail in the Federal and State Courts." In order to effect such a reform in the federal courts the A.B.A. had gone on to recommend specifically that section 914 of the federal Revised Statutes be repealed and appropriate new legislation passed by Congress. The Greenwood meeting also resolved to petition Mississippi's congressional delegation to work toward that end. But when the 1915 meeting assembled at Vicksburg, no progress had been made. Once again the Association voted its support for the idea. Its members also passed a resolution calling on the state Legislature, "in the interest of our state's commercial and industrial development . . . and to put us on a parity with practically all other English-speaking countries," to pass the Uniform Negotiable Instruments Law. Drafted by the American Law Institute with the encouragement of the A.B.A., the measure had already been adopted by forty-six states and territories. Washington was not yet ready to accept uniform procedure, but in April, 1916, the Mississippi Legislature did pass the act "to make the law of negotiable instruments uniform."[21]

A radical proposal made by Chief Justice Sydney Smith in his presidential address delivered at the opening session of the 1915 meeting was not destined to meet with the same success. The chief justice called for passage of a "Statewide Judicature Act" which would consolidate all of the state's existing courts into one "General Court of Judicature." The new consolidated court would have

---

20. Sunderland, pp. 87–88.
21. *Miss. Laws* (1916), c. 244.

three permanent divisions: the court of appeal, the superior court, and the county courts—one in each county. Suggested by the British Judicature Acts of 1873 and 1876 which had combined England's various high courts into a single "High Court of Judicature," the idea had been developed and promoted by the American Judicature Society founded in 1913 in Chicago. The avowed aim of the A.J.S., which had very close ties with the A.B.A., was to co-ordinate "the efforts of bar associations and individual lawyers throughout the country" in order to "assist the profession in expressing itself effectively in anticipated changes in courts and procedure." Its national officers, several of whom were connected with the University of Chicago Law School, worked with each individual state through a local "advisory council." In 1915 the members of the Mississippi advisory council were Monroe McLurg, Clayton D. Potter, W. D. Anderson, Percy Bell, and Chief Justice Smith.[22]

After hearing Smith's proposal, the members present voted to appoint a committee of five, chaired by D. W. Houston and including Greenville's Percy Bell, to consider its implications and report back to the meeting. Presumably they discussed the matter over lunch, for they were ready with their report at the afternoon session. Though they had only considered it briefly, they said, they were "favorably impressed by numerous features of the projected plan and realize[d] the weight and importance of the adoption by England of a similar system, the value of the recommendation by the American Judicature Society as well as our able and learned president and Chief Justice." Nevertheless, it obviously needed much more study by all the Association's members before it was finally voted on. Therefore they suggested referring the proposal to a special committee who would study it in depth and report to the next annual meeting.

At the 1916 meeting in Laurel, the members were told by the Standing Committee on Jurisprudence and Law Reform for the preceding year that they had considered and "heartily approved"

22. *Proc.* (1915), pp. 52–53.

President Smith's proposal. And G. G. Lyell of Jackson, chairman of the "Special committee on the retiring president's address," reported that his group favored it in principal also. One of their number in fact, V. A. Griffith of Gulfport, had gone so far as to prepare a draft statute that adapted the scheme to Mississippi's particular circumstances, needs, and traditions—for example using the term "district courts" in place of "county courts." Nevertheless, a majority of the committee felt that, since the proposed plan involved "changes in our judicial system that are so far reaching and fundamental" and since the Legislature would not meet in regular session again until 1918, it would be wise to devote at least one more year to studying and discussing all of its ramifications. The A.J.S. itself was reported to be still working on the plan, refining it further; and several A.B.A. committees were also still considering various aspects of it. So the whole question was referred to another special committee. This one was chaired by V. A. Griffith and included once again Percy Bell.

The 1917 meeting, at Greenville, after a brief discussion of it, referred the matter back once again for further study, this time to a special committee of twelve. On a motion by Professor Somerville the same committee was also asked to consider and report on the propriety of abolishing the distinction between common law and equity in Mississippi, as the Judicature Acts had done in England and as Vice-President R. B. Campbell had first suggested to the Association in 1910. A few weeks later an unsigned article entitled "A Unified Court for Mississippi" appeared in the very first issue of the *Journal of the American Judicature Society*.[23] It reported that, although one Supreme Court justice had denounced the plan as "an attempt to sell the people of the state into judicial slavery," majority opinion in the Bar Association favored it and it should receive final endorsement in 1918. The 1918 committee report—supposed to be the final one—was indeed again favorable to the unified court proposal. But George H. Ethridge of Meridian, a self-taught lawyer then serving the state as an assistant attorney gen-

23. June, 1917, pp. 15–17.

eral, managed to persuade the Association members meeting in Jackson that it would only be fair to have the president appoint a committee of five members opposed to the idea who could draw up a list of the objections they felt ought to be considered. Ethridge was appointed chairman of the opposition group who were instructed to publish their views in the 1918 *Proceedings* and to be prepared to discuss them at the 1919 meeting.

So the unified court proposal of President Smith had been much discussed by Association members from 1915 to 1918 and was generally approved, but no progress had yet been made towards bringing it into being. Nor had any progress been made in the matter of getting a second federal judge for the state, although in 1912 and again in 1917 strongly worded resolutions had been passed pointing out that the machinery and staff were already available for two federal judges and urging the Mississippi delegation in Congress to do whatever had to be done to secure passage of the necessary legislation. Even the fact that by 1913, for the first time in many years, there was a Democratic majority in both houses of Congress and a Democratic president in the White House, Woodrow Wilson—who, as R. N. Miller rejoiced in his presidential address to the Association that year, was "a lawyer born of the best Southern blood and nurtured on the generous bosom of the South"—made no difference. Henry C. Niles of Kosciusko, a member of Mississippi's tiny Republican minority, continued to serve both the northern and the southern U.S. districts.

Progress in one area, however, could be celebrated at the 1918 meeting: William Hemingway's new *Mississippi Code* had just been published. Two years earlier, at the Laurel meeting, the Association had voted its endorsement of a plan for a new code announced by the Bobbs Merrill Company of Indianapolis. The following year, at Greenville, his colleagues learned that Hemingway, a Jackson attorney, was serving as editor of the work which was to be in two volumes. Not only would it be updated, he told them in a letter, but it would also be thoroughly annotated and much more comprehensively indexed than that of 1906. The 1906 code was generally regarded as very unsatisfactory, and the members in

1918 enthusiastically voted their "profound appreciation" for what Hemingway had achieved.

At the opening session on the morning of May 1, 1918, everything else was overshadowed by the fact that the United States for a little more than a year had been involved in World War I in Europe. A. A. Armistead in his presidential address opening the proceedings spent a lot of his time discussing the new espionage law enacted by Congress eleven months earlier. A telegram was read from the Association's former secretary-treasurer, James R. McDowell, who had resigned the previous December to go into the army and now was serving as judge advocate general at Camp Bowie in Texas. Of the 1275 members of the state bar listed in an appendix to the 1918 *Report*, forty-nine were noted as serving with the armed forces. A motion made by Professor Somerville pledging the Association's members to make available their influence and services "without fee or reward" to assist the government in the beneficent enforcement of the War Risk Insurance Act was passed unanimously by a standing vote. Specifically they would handle claims or adjustments sought by beneficiaries free of charge, see that the availability of free assistance was publicized, continue providing the free service as long as there was any need for it, and report to the A.B.A.'s Washington office the names of any claims agents, pension attorneys, or other persons known to be violating the spirit of the act. Furthermore, they pledged that they, and all the lawyers in the state, would make a similar effort to give effect to the provisions of the Soldiers and Sailors Civil Relief Act—"to the end that those who are engaged in military service may have their rights and claims protected, their property interests preserved, and the final adjudication of such matters deferred until their return."

An additional set of three motions by S. E. Travis of Hattiesburg, who the following day was to be elected president for 1918–19, also passed unanimously. The first said that the dues of members serving with the armed forces would be remitted for the duration of the war; the second, that the Association's surplus funds would be invested in liberty bonds and war savings stamps. The third took the form of a resolution that it was "the sense of the Association that the Imperial German Government committed the greatest crime ever committed against civilization in precipitating the world war now in progress" and that the United States would "commit a still greater crime against the present and future generations, should it fail to prosecute the war to a complete victory."

At the Association's annual banquet held on the evening of May 1 in the Edwards Hotel, Sarah B. McLean's Majestic Court orchestra played, among other items, the one-step, "It's a Long Way to Berlin But We'll Get There," and the French march, "Lorraine." And Mrs. Hamilton Sivley sang a song entitled, "When the Boys Come Home." At the final business session the following afternoon the members passed a resolution pledging their "loyal support and co-operation" to President Wilson and his administration, "heartily and enthusiastically" endorsing the government's war policies, war aims, and the measures it had recommended "for the energetic prosecution of the War, for the mobilization of all the resources of the nation," and applauding it for its determination "to fight to a finish until the World is made safe for Democracy." Four days later President Wilson's private secretary, J. P. Tumulty, wrote from Washington to Secretary-Treasurer F. M. West in Jackson to thank him on behalf of the President for the Association's pledge of support.[24]

World War I brought about many changes. The western world, including Mississippi, would never be quite the same again. In the proceedings of the Bar Association meeting of 1918 one can see signs of some of those changes. For one thing the proceedings were issued for the first time since 1906 in a paperback cover at a cost of $352.10 for 500 copies as compared to $410.80 for the same number of hardcover copies in 1917. Presumably a scarcity of high-quality paper caused the changeover rather than a desire to save money, for the state's economy was booming. The outbreak of the war in Europe in 1914 had caused a great demand for Mississippi's agricultural products and therefore their prices had soared. New

24. *Proc.* (1918), p. 14.

processing plants were built. The state's climate made it a desirable location for army training facilities. A network of paved highways, to allow trucks to take goods to market quickly and to facilitate troop movements, was under construction.[25]

Mississippi's black majority, as well as its white minority, were making more money; and the war gave many Mississippi blacks for the first time an opportunity to leave their homes, to serve in the armed forces, or work in northern factories in locations where there were no humiliating "Jim Crow" laws. And, conversely, some Mississippi whites who volunteered for military service found themselves having to live and work with blacks on a basis of equality such as they had never experienced in their lives before. The State Bar list published as an appendix to the 1918 *Proceedings* includes the names of eleven "colored" attorneys, but of course none of them belonged to the Association.[26] And one of the resolutions addressed to President Wilson at the final business session on May 2, 1918, asked him to intervene in the case of Reserve Captain Eugene C. Rowan who was in a military prison at Camp Pike, Arkansas, after being found guilty by a court martial on a charge of disobeying orders. Captain Rowan's offense, as the resolution noted, had consisted of refusing "to allow his company to be drilled under his command alongside of negro troops in the same formation, and to stand in retreat should[er] to shoulder with negroes." For him to have done so, said the resolution, "would have destroyed the esprit de corps, and morale of Southern soldiers, and lessened their efficiency and patriotism." The resolution concluded with the statement that "Captain Rowan has been guided in his conduct by the highest purposes and, if punished at all, only the lightest penalty provided in such cases should be imposed." On May 7, J. P. Tumulty wrote once again to Secretary West informing him that the President had instructed him to acknowledge receipt of the resolution concerning Captain Rowan and that the matter had been referred to the Secretary of War.[27]

---

25. McLemore, II, 66–67, 286, 291, 319.

26. Six are listed in Hinds County, two each in Bolivar and Harrison counties, and one in Warren County.

27. *Proc.* (1918), p. 15.

Many women, as well as many blacks, got the opportunity to experience unaccustomed freedom from long-established social and economic conventions and restraints in World War I. By 1920 women in America would have the vote. And most members of the Mississippi Bar Association seem to have been in no way opposed to the new freedom sought by some women. It was at the 1918 meeting that the Association's first woman member, Miss Susie Blue Buchanan of Brandon, was admitted, apparently without controversy, to all the privileges of membership. According to the 1918 bar directory two other women, Miss Bessie Young of Grenada and Miss Leota Taylor of Jackson, were also practicing in the state by that time.[28]

In its first twelve years the Association had scored some achievements and solved some problems. But much that was desired had not been achieved, and many problems remained unsolved. By 1918 it was evident that the postwar era was going to produce some new ones; what remained to be seen was whether a voluntary selective state bar association could cope with them adequately and, at the same time, continue to maintain the honor and dignity of the legal profession in a changing Mississippi.

28. The 1915 bar directory, published with the *Proceedings* for that year, lists a Mrs. Lucy H. Greaves in Gulfport, but her name does not appear in subsequent directories. Bessie Young was apparently the first woman to graduate from the University of Mississippi law school in 1915. Miss Linda Rives Brown of Meridian graduated with honors in 1916. See the University Archives.

III

The Last Years of the Bar Association

1919–1931

WHEN THE MEMBERS of the Bar Association assembled in Clarksdale for their fourteenth annual meeting on April 30, 1919, the First World War, though it had ended six months earlier, was still very much on their minds. Apparently no Association member had lost his life during the twenty months that Americans had been involved in the fighting in Europe, for the Obituaries and Memorials Committee had no report to make; however, a few had seen service overseas. M. E. White, a Columbus attorney, gave a talk on his experiences as a captain in the Army, and Professor Duke M. Kimbrough of the University Law School told what it had been like working in France as a Y.M.C.A. official.[1] Kimbrough later moved a resolution, which the members unanimously adopted, expressing support for the erection in Jackson of "a permanent and worthy memorial to Mississippi's soldiers, sailors, and other war workers."

In his presidential address, delivered at the opening session in the Marion Theater, S. E. Travis of Hattiesburg emphasized that many of those lawyers who had stayed at home had also played an important part in the successful war effort. A lot of them had cheerfully made their services available free of charge at the government's request. Some had lost well-paid positions in private corporations that were taken over by the government. Nearly all

1. Kimbrough had served as third district chancellor from 1911 to 1913, when he replaced T. C. Somerville as senior law professor on the latter's retirement. In 1920 he left the law school to go into private practice in Boulder, Colo. See *Miss. LJ*, I (1928–29), 174–75.

had suffered a considerable decline in their professional incomes. But their sacrifices had not gone entirely unnoticed or unappreciated. An editorial published some three weeks earlier in Travis's own hometown newspaper, the *Hattiesburg American*, had remarked: "Many are the people who have given unselfishly of their time and money to the service of the country, and have cheerfully borne heavy burdens, but the *American* has known no class of men more loyal in this respect than the lawyers."

A. Mitchell Palmer of Pennsylvania, Attorney General of the United States, giving the annual address, reported on his work as the federal government's Alien Property Custodian from October, 1917, to March, 1919 and cited another important contribution that the legal profession had made to the war effort. The nearly 140,000 members of the American Bar, he recalled, had been of tremendous assistance in carrying out his important task by making available to him and his staff their considerable collective knowledge of transactions and conveyances entered into by enemy nationals and enemy-owned corporations who were attempting to evade the provisions of the Trading with the Enemy Act by making it difficult to determine the real owners of certain properties. In fact, Palmer concluded, his had been "one of the few agencies where the lawyer as such could wield an effective blow in his country's cause."

But the war was over; the victory had been won; and Palmer would soon be making a reputation for himself as a "red-baiter." Meanwhile, some members of the Mississippi Bar were beginning to wonder what life in the 1920s would be like for returning G.I.'s and other Mississippians. George F. Maynard, in a speech welcoming the Association to Clarksdale, reminded them that: "It is the duty . . . of our wise men and lawyers to have laws enacted which will tend to secure homes and living wages for our laborers. These are not merely socialistic doctrines. They are demands for remedy against evils which are now drawing the attention of all thinking men." Later the same day, W. J. Pack of Laurel, a self-taught lawyer who was destined to serve as a state Supreme Court justice (1928–29), read to his colleagues a paper in which he thoroughly discussed, and generally favored, passage of a workmen's compensation law for Mississippi similar to those already in effect in thirty-eight other states. Those present were persuaded, and they voted the following day to set up a three-man committee headed by Pack to work for passage of such a law by the Legislature. Not until 1948, however, would Mississippi's lawmakers enact legislation regulating damages for injuries suffered by employees while on the job without consideration of negligence or fault.[2]

Meanwhile, the 1920s and 1930s were a time of severe financial hardship for many people in the state. While most Americans enjoyed a kind of hectic prosperity during the decade from 1919 to 1929, Mississippi, with an economy based almost entirely on agriculture and particularly on the production of a single crop (cotton), in common with some of the other farming areas of the country suffered from a recession. Because production had been greatly stepped-up to meet wartime demand, markets became glutted, causing prices to plummet below prewar levels. Cotton peaked at 35.54 cents a pound in 1919, but in 1920 dropped to 15.84 cents, and the average price through the 1920s was only 17.66 cents. The beginning of a nationwide depression at the end of the decade made a bad situation in Mississippi much worse. In 1931 cotton fetched only 5.66 cents a pound.[3]

In the poor economic climate of the 1920s most Mississippians could not have had much money to spare for attorneys' fees. Nevertheless, the number of licensed lawyers in the state increased slightly, from just under 1300 in 1918 to about 1400 in 1928.[4] During the same period the membership of the Bar Association apparently expanded from a low of 290 in 1921 to a high of 520 in 1928–29, or twice what it had been ten years before.[5] But the published membership lists are rather misleading. The attendance at annual meetings, always somewhere between 100 and 125, was

2. *Miss. Laws* (1948), c. 354.
3. McLemore, II, 75, 94.
4. *Miss. LJ*, II (1929–30), 1.
5. The membership lists were published each year in the *Proceedings*.

somewhat less than it had been a decade earlier and did not increase in spite of the apparent increase in membership.

At the 1924 meeting there was a departure from the 1906 decision to interpret article XV of the by-laws very strictly by limiting honorary membership in the Association to the United States district judge and the state's Supreme Court justices, circuit judges, and chancellors. After R. E. L. Saner of Dallas, president of the American Bar Association, had delivered a stirring annual address on the topic, "Has America Outgrown the Constitution?," on a motion by A. W. Shands it was voted unanimously to make him an "honorary life member of the Mississippi State Bar Association." The following year, on a motion by E. F. Noel, former United States Senator John Sharpe Williams (1908–22), retired United States judge Charles B. Howry,[6] and all other Confederate veterans belonging to the Association were made "life members." A further motion conferred the same status on E. J. Bowers, a retired Gulfport attorney who had had a long and distinguished career at the bar. In 1928, after hearing his annual address "On the Constitution," the members resolved to make Judge C. B. Ames of Oklahoma, an 1892 University of Mississippi Law School graduate, a second "Honorary Life Member" along with Saner.

Honorary or life membership excused one from paying annual dues. Many ordinary members, however, seem to have paid theirs very irregularly. Although article XII of the by-laws stated that any member who had not paid his dues by March 1 of any year was to be removed immediately from the list of members by the Executive Committee, the rule was never enforced. At the 1925 annual meeting, in Laurel, a resolution was passed stating that any member who failed to pay his dues for *two successive* years was to be dropped automatically from the rolls. Presumably that meant that one could pay every other year only and still remain in good standing. In May, 1929, at Clarksdale, President George W. Currie

6. For an account of Judge Howry's career, see Rowland, *Courts*, pp. 156–78. His home in Oxford, now named "Fiddler's Folly," is regularly included in the Oxford Pilgrimage each April.

of Hattiesburg told the members that only those "lawyers residing in the immediate section of the annual meeting usually attend and pay their dues." The genuinely active membership he assessed at around 300.

When, just five months later, all of America was affected by the beginning of the Depression era, its effects on the Mississippi State Bar Association were soon very evident. The number of members dropped to 275 in 1930, and by the time of the 1931 meeting to 185. For those who believed in the importance of the Bar Association and the value of the work it was doing, therefore, the "roaring twenties" was often a time of disappointment and frustration. More and more of them probably found themselves agreeing with Jeff Truly's recommendation in his speech at the 1921 meeting "that it should not only be permitted, but made mandatory, that every practicing lawyer in the State should be a member of the State Bar Association. . . ."

All of those who served terms as president of the Association from 1919 to 1932 were, of course, outstanding members of their profession, but three of them deserve special mention. Judge Stone Deavours (1924–25) of Laurel had served as second district chancellor from 1900 to 1904 before returning to private practice in his hometown. While president he attended the 1924 Democratic National Convention as a member of the Mississippi delegation. His predecessor, R. H. Thompson (1923–24) of Jackson, had a third of a century earlier served a term (1890–91) as president of the previous State Bar Association and by the 1920s was generally revered as the grand old man of the legal profession in Mississippi. A delegate to the Constitutional Convention of 1890 from Lincoln and Jefferson counties, he had been chosen to chair the committee of lawyers who drafted the 1892 *Code*. From 1900 to 1905 he served as a member of the New Capitol commission and in 1917 was appointed president of the board of trustees of the state's Department of Archives and History. T. C. Kimbrough (1929–30), originally from West Point, was probably the single most influential member of the Mississippi Bar in the 1920s and 1930s. Having served a brief term in 1914 as circuit judge for the sixteenth district, in

1920 he succeeded Duke M. Kimbrough (not apparently a close relative) as the second law professor at the University of Mississippi. He was appointed dean of the law school in 1921, and he was to spend the remaining quarter-century of his life working energetically, persistently, and successfully to raise the level of educational and professional preparedness of Mississippi lawyers.[7] Frequently he would have to ask the Bar Association for help in doing so, and usually he got it.

The secretary-treasurership of the Association continued to be held by F. M. West until 1921 when Chalmers Potter, a young Jackson attorney, was elected to the position. Potter, a 1916 graduate of the University Law School, had served as an officer with the American Expeditionary Force in Europe before returning home to practice law in the state capital. In 1922 he was appointed an assistant United States attorney in Jackson.[8] Evidently, however, he was no accountant, or else he was simply too busy to devote much time to the Association's finances; for during the three years that he held office no financial reports were given at the annual meetings or printed in the proceedings.

Some members must have begun to worry about the situation, and Potter himself finally asked for help. On the opening day of the 1924 annual meeting in Jackson a motion passed appointing a special three-man committee, chaired by A. W. Shands, "to investigate the financial affairs of the Association and report . . . on the following day." Their report, when it came, was a depressing one. While some 300 members were paying their dues regularly, which meant an anticipated income of $1,500 for 1924, the estimated expenses for the year were $1,510, and some unpaid debts were still pending, so that a total deficit of a little over $400 could be anticipated. The Hinds County Bar Association had voluntarily contributed $150, and R. L. McLaurin of Vicksburg had made a personal contribution of $25; but Hardin H. Brooks' proposal that

7. Rowland, *Courts*, pp. 196–246, 252, 263. Rowland, *Mississippi*, III, 1219–20; IV, 209–10, 228–32. George H. Ethridge, *Mississippi, A History* (4 vols.; Jackson, n.d.), III, 1397–1403. *Miss. LJ*, I (1928–29), 175. Kirwan, pp. 280–81.

8. Rowland, *Mississippi*, III, 180.

the problem be solved by every one of the hundred-odd members present paying five dollars to the treasurer met with a mixed reception.

There is no way of ascertaining how many of those present did make the extra payment. But J. T. Brown of Jackson, who had audited Potter's books for Shands' committee, was elected secretary-treasurer. A banking executive as well as a lawyer, Brown was evidently the right man for the job.[9] At the 1925 meeting he presented a full financial report which informed those present that all past-due debts had been paid off and that, although expenses for the year just past had exceeded $1,800, there was a healthy cash balance of over a thousand dollars on hand. Brown continued to hold the office until 1928 when he was succeeded by Louis M. Jiggitts, who was destined to play a role second in importance only to that of Dean Kimbrough in the Association in the 1930s.

Annual meetings from 1919 to 1931 continued to be held each year on the Wednesday and Thursday after the first Monday in May. The only two exceptions were in 1925, when for some unexplained reason the Executive Committee scheduled the meeting for May 28–29, and in 1927 when, because of the severe floods that had devastated the Delta that spring, the meeting was postponed until June 10–11. The practice of meeting in different cities around the state was also continued, though with some changes in the cities chosen. The choice was always made by a vote taken at the final business session on Thursday afternoon, and usually lawyers from two or three towns would extend invitations from their communities. No doubt the businessmen of any of Mississippi's larger towns in the 1920s would have been delighted to attract a convention of some two or three hundred well-to-do, professional people. Such a gathering, for two or three days and nights, would have represented a considerable financial windfall. The Gulf Coast, of course, continued to be the favorite meeting place. Biloxi acted as

---

9. During the 1920s Brown was attorney for the State Banking Department and in 1933 was appointed President of the Capital National Bank (now the First National Bank) in Jackson. See J. T. Brown, *A Story of Banking in Mississippi* (New York: Newcomen Society in North America, 1961), p. 6.

the host city on three occasions, in 1923, 1926, and 1930, and Gulfport once, in 1928. Jackson was another obvious location, and the Association again went there twice, in 1924 and 1928. Natchez, West Point, Hattiesburg, Greenwood, and Greenville, all of which had acted as host cities in 1907–1918, though they were on occasion nominated, never actually got to host a meeting in this later period. Three new locations visited were Clarksdale in 1919 and 1929, Vicksburg in 1922, and Browns Wells Health Resort in Copiah County in 1921. Meridian was another city visited twice, in 1920 and 1931, and Laurel acted as host once, in 1925.

In 1922, at Vicksburg, for the first time a stenographic record of the proceedings was kept. As a result, from that year onward the annual meetings became much more vividly real for the historian. With all of the brief comments, interjections, and asides included, it is far easier to assess the shifting moods of the meetings and the impact of various influential personalities on the members' deliberations. It was also at Vicksburg in 1922 that, in addition to the customary steamboat excursion on the river, the innovation was introduced of offering members and their families an opportunity to go on an automobile outing into the surrounding countryside. This agreeable practice became a regular feature of the meetings until the outbreak of World War II when gasoline rationing put an end to it. Yet another innovation was begun at Gulfport in 1928 when the practice of holding a formal ball on the first night of the meeting was initiated.

Music of one kind or another was always a major feature of the meetings between the two world wars. Local ladies of talent were customarily invited to sing or play something appropriate to the occasion at the opening ceremonies. And there was usually music at the annual dinner also. In 1926, after the meal at the Buena Vista Hotel in Biloxi, "Miss Doyle" demonstrated the Charleston, and other girls from Gulf Park Junior College performed two "aesthetic dances."

The fact that selling liquor was prohibited not just by state statute but by an amendment to the U.S. Constitution was an important consideration at all of the annual meetings during the twenties. The state Legislature, at the urging of Governor Theodore Bilbo, in the second week of January, 1918, had made Mississippi the very first state to endorse the "National Prohibition Amendment."[10] A. A. Armistead, however, in his presidential address at the annual meeting four months later, had expressed the fear that, because it "would delegate to the Federal Government the right to regulate internal affairs of the sovereign states," transferring to Washington in fact "the police power of the several states over this question," the amendment represented a very severe blow to the concept of states' rights. But the following year, President Travis applauded the new measure, by then already in force. He was, he claimed, all in favor of states' rights, and considered himself to be a strict constructionist; nevertheless it had to be remembered that "the liquor traffic has never been simply a local question and has never recognized state boundaries." Therefore it could only be dealt with on a national basis, by national legislation. And three years later President George J. Leftwich of Aberdeen optimistically forecast that "the wealth formerly wasted in the unnecessary use of intoxicants and now saved to the nation by universal prohibition, if conserved, will in a few years discharge the debt created by the world war, both principal and interest." In fact, of course, the federal government was compelled to spend vast amounts of additional money on attempts to enforce prohibition, attempts that were almost totally futile. It is true that alcoholic beverages did disappear completely from the Bar Association's annual dinner menus. "Roman Punch" was offered at Clarksdale in 1919 and "California Sherry" at Laurel in 1925, but presumably they were non-alcoholic or low-alcohol beverages.

At the same time, it is obvious, even from the published proceedings, that quantities of intoxicants were consumed at every annual meeting. In 1924 J. N. Flowers, in his speech of welcome delivered on behalf of the Hinds County Bar, remarked that "in the last few years this standard form of welcoming address has invariably had added to it something about refreshments that are

10. McLemore, II, 68–70.

not put on the menu cards, and that the waiters themselves are not supposed to talk about." He went on to caution that in Jackson both the officers of the law and the citizenry took prohibition seriously. If so, they seem to have been atypical, or perhaps they simply did not feel such an urgent need to attract conventions to their town. At Laurel the next year the Mayor told Association members: "There is to be no interference allowed with any of your activities, or your business or pastimes." In fact, he confided, he had "called off nearly all the policemen in the city while the lawyers are here." And in 1926 Mayor Scott of Biloxi assured members: "If perchance you do need a little something 'on the cob,' as has been suggested," it could certainly be provided, or, "if you brought your own samples along with you," that was fine too. Many local officials, in fact, and many members of the bar, seem to have been of the same mind as Judge Joseph W. Bailey of Texas who in the 1923 annual address, speaking on the topic "Our Federal Government," remarked: "It is infinitely better that a few weak men should debase themselves by an over-use of liquor, than it is that all men should be subjected to the arbitrary power of irresponsible federal agents."

President Leftwich in the same speech in which he hailed the passage of the Eighteenth (prohibition) Amendment also spoke approvingly of the Nineteenth Amendment which had given votes to women in 1920. While it had to be admitted, he observed, that woman "is more sentimental, more impulsive, perhaps more fickle in her aims and purposes," yet "on the whole she is more ethical." And because she is "largely influenced by moral motives," he was confident that she "will be a militant protagonist of law enforcement." It was "perfectly plain that her early entry into the jury box as well as occasionally into civil office" was "inevitable," he concluded. He only hoped that "her new duties will not detract from her homemaking qualities."

As things turned out, it would be nearly fifty more years before the state constitution was amended so as to allow women into Mississippi jury boxes. But less than two years after Leftwich's cautious commendation of political rights for women, Mrs. Nellie

Nugent Somerville, whose husband Robert N. Somerville of Cleveland was a Bar Association member, was to be elected to the state Legislature from Washington County, taking her seat in January, 1924.[11] As we have already seen, Susie Blue Buchanan of Brandon had been admitted as the first woman member of the Bar Association in 1918. Sara L. Buchanan of Booneville was admitted in 1921, and Lucy Somerville of Cleveland, Nellie Nugent Somerville's daughter, in 1923. In 1924, the same year that her mother first sat in the Legislature, Miss Somerville became the first woman ever formally to address the Association, reading a paper on "Laws about Lawyers."

She remarked in her paper that there were then some 1800 female lawyers in America or about 1.5 percent of a total of 120,000. Mississippi with only about half a dozen out of some 1300, or about 0.45 percent, was far below the national average, therefore; but certainly the Bar Association exhibited no overt male chauvinism. Sara Buchanan in 1922 had been chosen as one of the members of the standing committee on Legal Education and Admission to the Bar, and in 1924 Miss Somerville went as one of the three officials delegates to the A.B.A. annual meeting held in the autumn in Philadelphia. In 1926 a woman lawyer from out-of-state, Mrs. Anna Dickie Olesen of Minnesota, spoke to the Association on behalf of the proposal for a St. Lawrence-Great Lakes waterway which she hoped the members would urge Mississippi's congressional delegation to support.

But if Mississippi's women made some progress in the 1920s, the state's blacks, who still constituted a small majority of her population,[12] did not. It is impossible to tell how many black law-

---

11. *Miss. Laws* (1968), cc. 335–36. McLemore, II, 79. Nellie Nugent Somerville was the daughter of William L. Nugent and Eleanor Smith Nugent. William's letters written to Eleanor during the Civil War have recently been published by the University Press of Mississippi. See William M. Cash and Lucy Somerville Howorth, eds., *My Dear Nellie* (Jackson, 1977). R. N. Somerville, husband of Nellie and father of Lucy, was a cousin of Dean T. H. Somerville of the University of Mississippi Law School.

12. According to the 1920 U.S. census, Mississippi's population included 953,184 blacks, 853,962 whites, and 1,472 persons of other races. See McLemore, II, 75.

yers were practicing in the state during the decade because the published bar lists no longer distinguished members by race, but probably there were fewer than ten.[13] Due to the depressed condition of the state's economy between the world wars, the poor-white segment of the population, finding themselves frustratingly close to the bottom of the socio-economic ladder, came to be more than ever resentful of black competition for jobs, land, and social services. Many of them consequently developed a virulent hatred for their colored fellow-citizens, a fact which, since very few blacks were enfranchised, certain of the state's more demagogic politicians were quick to take advantage of. All office-holders, or would-be office-holders, had to take it into account. Members of the Bar Association, however, belonging as they did to the state's professional, upper-class *élite*, tended to regard blacks with benevolent paternalism and apparently felt that, though they might not be in all respects the equals of whites, they were entitled to the equal protection of the law.

State Supreme Court Associate Justice J. B. Holden, in his presidential address delivered at the annual meeting in Biloxi in 1923, rejoiced at the defeat of the Harding administration's antilynching (Dyer) bill which had been killed by a southern filibuster in the Senate the previous December. Even had it passed, he asserted, it must have been declared unconstitutional in the federal courts. But, he conceded, it had to be admitted that "our Northern brethren" had some cause for their agitation, for lynching was a serious national problem and it was especially prevalent in the South. Though Holden did not say so, Mississippi in fact had been the scene of more lynchings than any other state during the preceding fifty years.[14] The way to end the agitation, Holden suggested, was to remove its cause. "Is it not time," he asked, "that the members of the legal profession especially in the Southern states make a

13. There were eleven in 1918 (see p. 42 herein), but only five on the 1941 list.

14. Walter White, *Rope and Faggot* (New York: Arno Press, 1969), pp. 234–36. There were 561 lynchings in Mississippi, 1882–1927, 517 of the victims being black.

radical effort toward the end that all persons charged with crime be given a fair trial under the process of law?"

It must have been very gratifying for the members when later on at the same meeting a delegation of blacks, led by the principal of the local "Colored School," presented to them a bouquet of flowers accompanied by a note which read in part: "Please accept this as a faint token of honor and appreciation for your presence in the City. We know the destiny of this great country is in your hands." In response President Holden observed:

> We like to have the respect of the colored people, and every lawyer, in my experience, had stood for a square deal before the law for the colored race. And often, as we know, in the last ditch, the colored man has only one friend, and that is his lawyer. These sentiments, no doubt have moved the colored people to make this presentation. . . .

The lynchings continued, however. Altogether there were seventeen in Mississippi in the four-year period, 1924–27, sixteen of the victims being blacks. Only Florida, with nineteen, had more. J. N. Flowers, President of the Bar Association from 1925 to 1926, seems to have been the moving spirit behind a booklet published in Jackson in December, 1925, entitled *Mississippi and the Mob.*[15] In his presidential address at Biloxi the following May, he commented that he and a number of other citizens had contributed to the publication intending that it should be "circulated among the people of this state with a view to arousing the public conscience to the gravity of this disgrace." He himself, he said, had contributed to it "not as president of this Association but solely as a citizen of Mississippi."

In fact, however, his own nine-page "Introductory Statement" made up much the largest single segment of the booklet; and, although it included condemnations of lynching from such notable

15. Printed by the Jackson Printing Co. (n.d.). Although the booklet has been attributed to the Bar Association, President Flowers' speech in 1926 makes it clear that it was not an Association publication and the financial report for 1925–26 does not list a payment for any such publication.

Mississippians as Methodist Bishop Charles B. Galloway and Chancellor Hume of the University, the bulk of it consisted of statements from prominent members of the bench and bar. Chief Justice Sydney Smith and Associate Justices Holden, J. G. McGowen, W. D. Anderson, and George H. Ethridge, as well as W. Webb Venable, George J. Leftwich, A. T. Stovall, J. S. Sexton, Stone Deavours, Tom Brady, Jr., and others were quoted. The booklet's general theme was that lynchings could be ended if all decent citizens would join in condemning them and if sheriffs and other law enforcement officers always made it clear that lynching attempts would be resisted with armed force if necessary. "Who," Flowers asked in his introduction, "has ever heard of a member of a mob in this state being killed or wounded while acting in the mob enterprise?" He advocated that section 175 of the state Code be amended so as "to authorize the legislature under the usual conditions as to notice and hearing to provide that the occurrence of a lynching in the county would ipso facto disqualify and remove from office the sheriff."

A year later, at the 1927 meeting in Jackson, a resolution was unanimously adopted by a standing vote of the members which congratulated those state, county, and local officials who "by their diligence had prevented a lynching" during the preceding twelve months. The Bar Association itself can perhaps take some of the credit for the fact that lynchings every year thereafter became less common in Mississippi, finally ceasing altogether in the 1950s, though it must be admitted that their anti-lynching campaign was launched originally because of pressure from outside the state and above all from the fear of federal government intervention.

The federal government was an outside force that very much concerned the members of the State Bar in the 1920's. They were particularly resentful, as we have seen, of the large-scale intrusion into the area of liquor prohibition enforcement by Treasury Department agents operating under the provisions of the Volstead Act of 1919. In the 1923 annual address Joseph W. Bailey of Texas complained bitterly that "by prostituting the power to levy taxes, and by stretching the power to regulate commerce, Congress has enacted many laws which it had no right to enact." Most Mississippi lawyers, to judge from their speeches printed in the Association's *Proceedings*, agreed with him. They were only thankful that the United States Supreme Court, "which," said R. V. Fletcher of Chicago in the 1925 annual address, "has always been the chief guardian of our liberties, and the best hope for the permanence of our institutions," could usually be relied on to curb the worst excesses of power-hungry Washington officials.

The other major outside influence, one much less resented, was the American Bar Association. In 1919 the chairman of the A.B.A.'s Membership Committee complained, in a letter read to the annual meeting at Clarksdale, that fewer than six percent (eighty) of Mississippi's lawyers were paying the eight dollars annual dues to belong to the national professional group. He appealed to each one who was a member to try to recruit two or three others. And the recruiting drive in fact was quite successful. By 1921 there were 92 members; by 1926 there were 126; and by 1931 there were 208 names on the published list. Mississippi attendance at A.B.A. annual meetings during the 1920's averaged ten, which was four more than the average for the previous decade. It was still true, however, that the state Association's formally elected delegates and alternates very rarely actually went. Rather the same small group of Mississippi lawyers tended to go nearly every year, while others went only once or twice. A. W. Shands, A. T. Stovall, and J. S. Sexton continued to go regularly, and W. S. Welch of Laurel, B. L. Jones of Jackson, and Gabe Jacobson of Meridian almost always went with them. The smallest delegation, only four, went to the 1922 meeting in San Francisco. Not surprisingly, the largest group, some 108, attended the Memphis meeting in 1929.[16] The interest in the A.B.A. aroused by the Memphis meeting probably explains to a considerable extent Mississippi's sizable increase in membership at the end of the decade.

16. A.B.A. *Annual Reports* (1919–1931), *passim*. Wickser, p. 419. The average attendance of ten, of course, does not include the Memphis meeting. Although Wickser says that 226 Mississippians attended the Memphis meeting, only 108 are listed as registrants in the A.B.A. *Report*.

The delivery of the annual address by R. E. L. Saner at Jackson in 1924 marked the first occasion ever that the president of the A.B.A. spoke to the Mississippi Bar Association. To the question posed by the title of his talk, "Has America Outgrown the Constitution?," his answer was no; he added, however, that there was a need "to beware of present day visionaries and to catch and hold fast to the vision of our Fathers." Two years earlier, as chairman of the A.B.A.'s newly-created American Citizenship Committee, Saner had presented a report to that organization's annual meeting at San Francisco on the need "to re-establish the Constitution of the United States in the minds and hearts of the people." The report went on to make several specific recommendations, all of which were enthusiastically endorsed by the national group.[17] And now, not only did the Mississippi Association vote to make Saner their first extraordinary honorary member, they also resolved to set up their own Citizenship Committee in order to carry out his and the A.B.A.'s recommendations in this state. The new committee was to be headed by the state's representative on the A.B.A. General Council as chairman with the state Bar Association's president for the year as vice-chairman. The secretary-treasurer, the members of the A.B.A. local council, and at least one other lawyer from each congressional district were to make up the membership.

For some reason that is not altogether clear from the *Proceedings*, the Citizenship Committee never did get listed in the Association's by-laws as one of the standing committees; but it did continue to exist as a "special committee" during the mid-1920s and was extremely busy. The active members in 1924–25 were J. S. Sexton, W. D. Anderson, L. B. Jones, George Leftwich, and Secretary-Treasurer Brown, all of whom, except for Brown, were frequent attenders at A.B.A. annual meetings. The A.B.A. campaign on Citizenship was aimed especially at two prime targets: foreign nationals living in America and students. Certainly foreign

17. *Who Was Who in America* (1847–1942), s.v. Saner, Robert E[dward] L[ee]. Sunderland, pp. 108–09.

nationals were understandably apt to be unfamiliar with the American constitutional tradition, and many had brought with them from the old world various extremist ideologies which no doubt had considerable appeal among the immigrant, factory-worker populations of the northern cities. And Mississippi lawyers worried about the problems they presented to the nation as a whole. George Leftwich in his presidential address at the 1922 meeting had praised the restrictive Alien Immigration Act of 1920 because so many of the immigrants were "arrogant socialists, bolshevists, industrial workers of the world, disciples of the Marxian theory of government, followers of Lenine [*sic*] and Trotsky," or else were "anarchists who believe in no government at all." A year earlier President Gabe Jacobson had commented that "the alien who does not approve of our system of government, and who preaches his disapproval and encourages resistance to it, should be promptly deported." But fewer than half of one percent of Mississippi's residents in the 1920s were foreign born.[18] So the Citizenship Committee concentrated its efforts on the youth of the state. Because of their efforts, the Superintendent of Education designated the week beginning April 20, 1925, as "Constitution Week" in Mississippi schools and colleges. Judges and members of the bar were invited to give special lectures on citizenship. Chancellor Allen Cox of Baldwyn spoke at the University at Oxford, and J. S. Sexton visited Mississippi College in Clinton. A Brookhaven schoolgirl got into the finals of the A.B.A.-sponsored national oratorical contest on aspects of the Constitution.[19] In 1927 the committee was able to report that, thanks to its efforts, a new textbook was being used for eleventh and twelfth grade government courses in Mississippi schools "wherein the study of the Constitution of the United States is made a special feature."

Under the American Constitution, with its basic principle of government by laws rather than by men, it is always essential that American lawyers be well trained in their profession and be im-

18. White, p. 237.
19. *Proc.* (1925), pp. 81–85.

bued with the very highest ethical standards; and both the A.B.A. and the Mississippi State Bar Association, as we have seen, from the very beginning have always been greatly concerned with the ethical standards of the legal profession. After 1912 both groups had the same code of ethics until 1929. At the Mississippi Association's annual meeting in Clarksdale in 1929, however, the standing committee on Professional Ethics reported that the A.B.A. at its 1928 meeting in Seattle had added thirteen new canons to its code.[20] Since all but one of the thirteen new rules either were already covered by the state's statute law or else referred to "conditions and practices that do not prevail to any extent, if at all, in Mississippi," the committee recommended that only that one—number 34 concerning the division of fees with non-lawyers—be adopted. Their recommendation was accepted with the result that the A.B.A. and Mississippi Codes of Ethics were no longer exactly identical. Copies of both codes were distributed to all the lawyers in the state.

The new dean of the University Law School, T. C. Kimbrough, firmly believed that the best time for lawyers to learn the accepted ethics of their profession was while they were still students. In 1922 he reported to the annual meeting at Vicksburg that, at his invitation, President George J. Leftwich had twice during the preceding year traveled from his home at Aberdeen to Oxford to lecture to law classes on "The Ethics of the Legal Profession." Kimbrough hoped, he said, that it would become the established practice for future presidents of the Association to do the same. President Leftwich enthusiastically endorsed the suggestion, and indeed President R. H. Thompson the following year gave a similar lecture. Also in 1923 the Association offered for the first time a medal to be awarded to the law student who wrote the best essay on the topic of legal ethics. At the 1924 meeting the first winner, Louis M. Jiggitts of Canton, was invited to read his paper to the members. Just four years later Jiggitts, a World War I veteran who had interrupted his law school career to go to Oxford University on a

20. See A.B.A. *Annual Report* (1928), pp. 778–82. Sunderland, pp. 112–13.

Rhodes Scholarship and earn a B.A. degree in Jurisprudence there in 1923, would become the Association's sixth secretary-treasurer.[21]

President Thompson, in his speech introducing Jiggitts, mentioned that there were 100 students enrolled in the law school. The type of education given to law students and the prerequisites for admission to the Bar were another major concern of the Association in the 1920s. At the 1922 meeting J. S. Sexton reported to the members on the results of an A.B.A.-sponsored conference on legal education that he had attended in Washington, D.C. three months earlier. Meeting in the Memorial Continental Hall the last week in February, he and his fellow delegates had passed resolutions recognizing the duty of organized bar associations to create and maintain high standards of legal education and bar admission and endorsing the standards in those two areas adopted by the A.B.A. at its 1921 annual meeting. The national group had stipulated that every candidate to enter the ranks of the legal profession should be a law school graduate and that every law school should require at least two years of undergraduate college work as a prerequisite for admission, should require every student to take three years of course work or the equivalent, should provide an "adequate" library, and should have a "sufficiency" of fulltime instructors on its staff. The A.B.A. had at the same time gone on record as being opposed to private law schools operated as commercial enterprises and had said that simply graduating from a law school should not confer the automatic right to be admitted to the bar.[22]

Mississippi, of course, did not comply with that last recommendation. Beginning with the very first class, which graduated in 1857, University Law School graduates had enjoyed the "diploma privilege" by which graduation meant automatic admission to the bar. The only other law school program in the state, the one at Millsaps College in Jackson, had been terminated in 1918 when almost its entire student body had left to go into the armed forces.[23] So during the 1920s the only other method of gaining admission to the state bar was by teaching oneself enough law to be able to

21. *America's Young Men*, III (1938–39), *s.v.* Jiggitts, Louis M.
22. Sunderland, pp. 145–46.
23. McLemore, II, 381.

pass the bar exam. The day after Sexton had given his report, J. D. Green, Jr., of Starkville, Secretary to the State Board of Bar Examiners, reported to members that most of the white applicants for admission had at least a high school education and that eighty percent had spent some time at a college or university. In fact, he concluded, the caliber of those entering the profession in Mississippi by the bar examination route was reasonably high. But in spite of what he had said and in spite of the contradiction with regard to the diploma privilege, before they adjourned the members passed a resolution expressing support for the standards adopted by the A.B.A. and the Washington conference.

The graduating class of the University Law School in 1925, at the suggestion of President Stone Deavours, were invited to attend the annual meeting in Laurel as guests of the Association. They heard George J. Leftwich report on behalf of the Legal Education Committee that their school met the A.B.A. standards in that it had three fulltime faculty members and a library of at least 6,000 volumes, that applicants in order to be admitted had to have completed at least the freshman and sophomore years of college, and that three years' fulltime residence with allowance for summer school attendance was required. Members could also take pride in the fact that in 1924 the fifty-two-member Association of American Law Schools, founded around the turn of the century with A.B.A. encouragement as an accrediting body for schools of law, had admitted the law school of the University of Mississippi with a "grade A" rating. But proud of the law school though they were, the committee nevertheless had some recommendations for its improvement. They were of the opinion that courses in bookkeeping, English and American history, and "political economy" (economics) would be desirable additions to the curriculum. But, most important of all, a new building was needed to provide the faculty and students with adequate office, classroom, and library space. The building then in use, they said, was "entirely inadequate."[24] The members responded by passing a resolution endorsing the com-

24. From 1911 to 1931 the law school was housed in the Gothic red-brick building on campus originally built to house the library, now known as the "Geology Building."

mittee's report and calling on the Legislature at its next meeting to vote sufficient funds to build a "more suitable" law school.

The 1926 session of the Legislature, however, failed to appropriate the money, and in 1927 members attending the annual meeting in Jackson learned some disturbing news from Dean Kimbrough. In November, 1926, an inspector from the A.A.L.S. had paid a visit to the law school, and at the annual conference of the accrediting body a month later, just after Christmas in Chicago, Kimbrough had been summoned before the executive committee. The inspector's report, they informed him, had not been favorable. Instead of the required 7,500 volumes, the University of Mississippi law library only contained 5,500. They had asked him, the dean recalled wryly, what his annual book budget amounted to, and he replied that it was only $500 per year; he noted, "Of course that created a great deal of amusement." Other shortcomings listed included the facts that many of the books in the library were shelved in such a way that it was difficult to get to them; that the library was sometimes used to teach classes so that other students could not use it; that, because there was only one regular classroom, all classes could not be held, as they were supposed to be, during the morning hours; and finally that some of the students admitted had had fewer than the required fifty hours of freshman and sophomore college work. The committee, therefore, informed Kimbrough that it had no choice but to recommend that his school be put on probation; this probation was in force. If steps were not soon taken to remedy the deficiencies, Kimbrough said, the law school would lose its A.A.L.S. accreditation altogether.[25] He and Chancellor Hume (who was also a trained lawyer and a member of the Bar Association) were determined to make every effort to prevent that from happening, but they needed the Association's support.

25. One cannot help wondering whether Dean Kimbrough may have himself requested the A.A.L.S. inspection which had such good results for his school in the long run, though the inspector's report also referred to some administrative shortcomings at the school which must have been very embarrassing for the dean; for full details of the report, see Hardy P. Graham, "Bilbo and the University of Mississippi (M.A. thesis, University of Mississippi, 1965), pp. 2–4.

They needed it, and they got it. A resolution was passed stating that "this Bar Association stands absolutely back of the Law School of the University of Mississippi in all its efforts." It was voted to send a copy of Dean Kimbrough's report to every member of the Legislature, and the president was instructed to appoint a special committee, with at least one member from each of the state's congressional districts, to work with the legislators and persuade them to act. R. E. Wilbourn of Meridian, the incoming president, appointed his predecessor, D. W. Houston, as chairman of the committee, which also included Stone Deavours, J. H. Price, Webb Venable, E. O. Sykes, A. J. McIntyre, future U.S. senator Wall Doxey of Holly Springs, and J. H. Currie. They and Wilbourn went to the University campus at Oxford for Homecoming Day, November 5, 1927, inspected the law school facilities for themselves, and drafted a memorial to the Legislature stressing the urgent need to do something about the deficiencies. The University's Alumni Association, meeting at the same time, voted their endorsement of the document. Then, during the next four months, the committee lobbied vigorously among the members of both legislative houses. President Wilbourn personally wrote a letter to each one of the lawmakers and to other men of influence.

All the hard work paid off. At the 1928 meeting in Gulfport, members heard of the happy outcome from President Wilbourn in his presidential address. Less than a week earlier, on April 26, the new governor, Theodore G. Bilbo (an Association member since 1925) had approved a special legislative appropriation of $1.6 million for new buildings and improvements at the University of Mississippi, and one of the major items included was $150,000 for the law school.[26] Reporting later Dean Kimbrough told the Association that $140,000 of the money allotted for the law school would be used to construct a new building and the remaining $10,000 would be used for buying books. The new facilities and the expanded li-

---

26. *Miss. Laws* (1928), c. 291. The largest single share of the appropriation, $200,000, was provided to build the Graduate School building (now Bondurant Hall).

brary would far exceed the minimum standards called for by the A.B.A., he concluded, and the school should have no trouble in winning back its grade A rating from the A.A.L.S.

The triumphant Kimbrough served as president of the Association in 1929–30. By the end of 1929 work had begun on the new law school building, "Lamar Hall." The A.A.L.S. restored the school's grade A rating in December, 1929, and by the end of 1930 its name had been added to the A.B.A.'s recently instituted list of approved schools. But whatever rejoicing there may have been was to be short-lived. By the time the A.B.A. voted to place his school on their approved list, Kimbrough was no longer its dean. Governor Bilbo, frustrated in his attempt to move the University to Jackson as the nucleus of a single, consolidated state university, nevertheless was determined to make substantial changes with regard to the institutions of higher education. By 1930 he had been able to place a majority of his supporters on the Board of Trustees and so began a series of extensive and highly controversial hirings and firings. At the University Chancellor Hume was removed from office; among other changes, Kimbrough was dismissed as dean of the law school, though permitted to remain on the faculty with substantially the same salary. The two other fulltime faculty members, Robert J. Farley and W. L. Hemingway, compiler of the *Code*, both of whom had openly opposed Bilbo politically, were fired outright.

Kimbrough's replacement as dean was Judge Stone Deavours, an outstanding jurist who had done much for the law school during the previous decade. Kimbrough himself remarked that, "if he were not to be Dean, there was no man in Mississippi under whom he would rather serve. . . ." The other new appointees were men of very high caliber also, and the State Bar Association had absolutely nothing to say at its 1931 annual meeting about a controversy in which some of their leading members were on opposing sides. But the A.A.L.S., after conducting an investigation, alleged that there had been blatant political interference in the administration of the law school and that Deavours, though he might be eminently qualified as a jurist, did not have the qualifications to be an educational administrator. In December, 1930, therefore, just one year after they had voted to reinstate the University of Mississippi, the accrediting body once again expunged it from their list of approved schools.[27]

Meanwhile, the deanship of the University law school was not the only subject over which members of the Bar Association were in disagreement. At the 1928 annual meeting the Committee on Legal Education and Admission to the Bar recommended petitioning the Legislature to mandate stricter requirements for candidates taking the bar examination. Their suggestion was that, within two years of the law being altered, candidates should have to have had at least two years of work at an accredited college or university and three years at an A.B.A. or A.A.L.S. approved law school, which would bring the state into compliance with the standards adopted by the A.B.A. in 1921. They also wanted the law changed so as to require all members of the board of bar examiners to have both a "literary" and a law degree from accredited institutions and to keep complete records of the exams given and of the candidates who took them, which would be available for public inspection in the Secretary of State's office. So controversial were these suggestions that the members postponed discussion of them till the next annual meeting, with the idea that in the meantime lawyers around the state could become familiar with them and give them serious consideration. In 1929, for the same reason, a decision on them was put off for yet another year.

The point of view of those who were opposed to the stricter standards was set forth by Supreme Court Justice George H. Ethridge, himself a self-taught lawyer, in an article in the February, 1930, issue of the *Mississippi Law Journal*. Those who approved of them, he suggested, did so "because they want to exclude from the profession all who have not been born with a 'golden spoon' in their mouths, and who have a prejudice against the self-educated men and women of the land." The committee's proposed changes, he concluded, "ought to be killed as surely as any other class legis-

27. For full details of the Bilbo "spoliation" of the law school, see Graham, pp. 48–53, 79, 88.

lation." Another article in the same issue, by Oxford Attorney Phil Stone, a Yale graduate, argued in favor of the changes. They would, he believed, "tend to bring about the greatest good of the greatest number of the people of Mississippi." "Democracies," he argued, "cannot afford to shun their experts, and cannot afford to have them badly trained."[28] But the issue was apparently too hot to handle for a Bar Association plagued with other problems and differences at a time of severe national economic depression. No more was heard of the recommendations, and the Committee on Legal Education and Admission to the Bar had no report to make at either the 1930 or 1931 annual meetings.

The founding in 1928 of the *Mississippi Law Journal*, which had provided Ethridge and Stone with a means whereby they could conveniently address themselves to all of the lawyers in the state, certainly must be counted as one of the major achievements of the Bar Association in the decade. As was the case with several of the Association's achievements in the period, the original impetus for it came from Dean Kimbrough. It was at his request that the 1922 annual meeting at Vicksburg listened to a proposal from Mr. McGill of the law school student body, the first law student ever to address the Association. He and the seventy or so other students ("including three girls") were interested in publishing, under the auspices of their honor society, the Blackstone Club, a "Mississippi Law Review" patterned after the law reviews put out by Harvard, Yale, Virginia, and other prestigious schools; they asked for the Association's help in getting the publication underway. The Board of Control, consisting of four Blackstone Club members and three other students, would soon be mailing out solicitations for subscriptions at two dollars per year to all the lawyers in the state. It was hoped that all members of the Association at least would subscribe and that they would also be willing to write articles for the "Review" when invited from time to time to do so. Apparently, however, the response to the mail-out was not encouraging. At the

28. *Miss. LJ*, II (1929–30), 276–92.

1923 meeting a committee was appointed to give further consideration to the "Question of Utilizing the Mississippi Law Review for the Advancement of the State Bar Association." A few issues of the Review reportedly put out by the students at the law school in 1923 and 1924 but then, because of financial difficulties, publication ceased.

But, four years later in 1928, R. E. Wilbourn, in his presidential address, told the members that he personally considered it "highly desirable" that the Association publish a law journal through which "it could more easily enlist and retain the interest of its individual members." Louis M. Jiggitts had proposed that they follow the example of Minnesota where the state Bar Association and the state University jointly published the monthly *Minnesota Law Review*. The idea was that the Mississippi Association and the University of Mississippi should issue a quarterly "law review and journal" along the same lines. The first issue each year, the summer one, could report the proceedings of that year's annual meeting. And, if the Association would only contribute what it already spent each year on printing the *Proceedings* ($534.54 for the 1927 meeting), that amount plus a small subscription should cover the publishing costs. Ultimate responsibility for the publication would be vested in a board of directors chaired by the law school dean and including the Bar Association's president, secretary, and Executive Committee members. A student editorial staff, picked by the board, would actually put it out under the supervision of the dean. Before adjourning on May 3, the members voted their approval of the idea.

In July, just two months later, issue number one of volume one of the *Mississippi Law Journal*, subtitled the "Journal of the State Bar Association," was run off the presses of the McCowat-Mercer printing house in Jackson, Tennessee. Consisting of the proceedings of the annual meeting, its title page contained the names of the directors, tactfully called the "Advisory Board," and of the student editors, headed by chief editor Dugas Shands of Cleveland. The Case Notes editor was John C. Satterfield of Port Gibson, a future president both of the Mississippi State Bar (1955–56) and of the American Bar Association (1961–62). The cost of an annual subscription was three dollars; a single copy sold for seventy-five cents. The bill for printing the issue, $491.85, was paid for by the Bar Association.

At the 1929 annual meeting editor Shands was able to report that the publication was off to a fair start. Four issues had appeared on schedule and had been mailed to 140 subscribers who were members of the Bar Association, as well as to forty-six more Mississippi lawyers who did not belong to the Association. Every one of the law students had paid his three dollars, and additional subscriptions had been received from eighty-six American law libraries and a dozen or so individuals and libraries overseas. Evidently those present were impressed for they voted to pay in the future $8.00 each year out of Association funds in return for each member getting a copy of every issue. Volume I had contained 468 pages. Volume II contained book reviews for the first time and was 492 pages in length. In 1931, however, "by reason of the recent depression," the subsidy was cut to $400 per year. Volume III had only 358 pages, and volume IV (1931–32) consisted of only three issues totalling 225 pages. Students and Bar Association members both must have wondered whether the *Mississippi Law Journal* would long survive.

Its well-being was of particular concern to those members of the Association who were concerned with the work of the American Law Institute founded in Philadelphia in 1923. The Institute's "Restatement" program was reported on at every annual meeting beginning in 1924. R. E. Wilbourn, in his presidential address in 1928, had pointed out the need to annotate the Restatements for Mississippi and to publish them for the benefit of the state's lawyers and legislators. Association members, he urged, should make themselves available to do the work of annotating, and the proposed new *Law Journal* could be the vehicle for publishing the work as it was done. At his suggestion a committee was appointed to coordinate and oversee the work, and a start was made in volume I of the *Journal*, which contained Chief Justice Smith's annotations on the Restatement of Torts.[29]

Restatements and other desirable law reforms had to be custom-tailored to the needs and circumstances of each individual state, as Henry Upton Sims, the second serving A.B.A. president ever to speak to the Association, pointed out in the 1930 annual address; in every case the group best suited to do the accommodating and adopting, he suggested, was the state bar association.[30] During the 1920s A. T. Stovall served as chairman of a group of Association members who served as a committee to work for acceptance by the state Legislature of the legislative proposals of the A.B.A.-backed Uniform Law Commission. Three of the proposed Uniform acts had been adopted in the previous decade: the Child Labor Act (1914), the Flag Act, and the Uniform Negotiable Instruments Act (both 1916). In 1920 the Legislature passed the Uniform Desertion and Non-Support Act and the Warehouse Receipts Act. But after that Stovall's committee had no further success. By 1931 Mississippi had still passed only those five of the forty-eight uniform acts which had been drawn up by the commissioners and endorsed by the A.B.A. since 1892.[31]

Undoubtedly the outstanding law-reform achievement of the Association during the decade was its successful lobbying of the Legislature to secure the passage of the Chancery Practice Act in 1924. Drawn up by Vergil A. Griffith, the draft act was presented to the Association and received its endorsement at the 1923 meeting in Biloxi. Its main result was to simplify chancery court procedures and make them much more flexible. That same year, 1924, chancery practice was made easier for the state's lawyers in another way by the publication of Griffith's treatise on *Mississippi Chancery Practice*, the second edition of which, published in 1950,

29. Pp. 236–267.

30. In introducing Sims, a Birmingham, Alabama, lawyer, the speaker pointed out that he was a native Mississippian and the son of a former lieutenant governor of the state, W. H. Sims (1878–82).

31. A.B.A. *Annual Report* (1931), pp. 827, 831.

remains the standard text on the subject to this day. Meanwhile, in 1921, W. L. Hemingway announced publication of a supplement to his *Code* covering new legislation enacted by the 1918 and 1920 sessions of the Legislature. In 1922 the Legislature adopted Hemingway's work as the official state code.[32]

In 1928, however, the newly-elected Legislature passed an act calling for a new, two-volume code; volume one was to contain "such laws of a criminal and civil nature as are most frequently used at the bar," and volume two "all the laws not embraced in volume one." Three members of the Association, Charles Lee Crum from the northern district, Supreme Court Justice V. A. Griffith from the southern district, and J. Morgan Stevens from the central district, were appointed by Governor Bilbo as commissioners to compile and annotate the new codification with Stevens acting as chairman. And a special committee was appointed by President George W. Currie to assist them in preparing the work, which was approved by the Legislature and published in 1930.

The full Legislature never would approve, however, a plan originally suggested by Dean Kimbrough and approved in 1928 by the House of Representatives for a "Permanent Commission on Law Revision." The idea was for the governor, attorney general, Supreme Court justices, and chairmen of the Judiciary Committees of both houses to choose three lawyers to serve as commissioners. The commissioners would have the job of compiling and presenting, at least sixty days before each legislation, "a report calling attention to such general statutes as [in their opinion] may be conflicting, of doubtful meaning, unconstitutional, obsolete or have a tendency unduly to complicate the administration of justice, or work a hardship or for any other reason requiring revision." At both the 1928 and 1929 annual meetings Association members voted approval of the concept, but a majority of both houses could

32. *Miss. Laws* (1924), c. 151. For a brief account of Griffith's life and achievements, see the article by his son-in-law, Chief Justice Robert Gillespie, in *JMH*, XXXVII (1975), 267–78. For an account of Hemingway's career, see *ibid.*, XXXVI (1974), 339–51. Hemingway Stadium on the University of Mississippi campus was named for him.

not be persuaded that such non-political input into the legislative process was a good idea.[33]

Meanwhile, the Association's members continued also to be very interested in the operations of the judicial branch of the state government during the 1920s. Here, as in other areas, there inevitably were frustrations. In spite of resolutions passed in 1919, 1921, and 1924, the Legislature could not be persuaded to pass a statute suspending the sitting of all state courts during the week of the annual meeting, "the principal thing that militates against our attendance here." Chief Justice Smith's proposal for a unified "General Court of Judicature" got nowhere. The entire concept was criticized in detail by Justice George Ethridge, R. H. Thompson, and others in a special supplement to the proceedings of the 1918 annual meeting, which argued that the unified court "might become burdensome and could serve no good purpose as we see it." However, in spite of what they had written, a majority at the 1919 annual meeting voted to continue the special committee of twelve set up two years earlier to study the idea and sell it to the Legislature; but no more is ever heard of the idea.

At the 1922 annual meeting members were concerned over an idea that had surfaced in the recently-concluded session of the Legislature for a constitutional amendment to make the state's elected officials subject to recall by petition. Justices and chancellors were specifically excepted, but the Legislature would be empowered to extend the procedure even to them if ever it chose to do so in the future. Approved by the lower house, the scheme had been killed in the Senate but might be revived. Back in 1911 the A.B.A. had voted its opposition to the notion of judicial recall, and it still had a committee in being whose function was to campaign against any extension of the practice. J. Morgan Stevens warned members against it in a strongly worded address entitled "Recall, Recount and Revolution." After listening to him, those present voted unanimously their opposition to the whole idea. The legislation, of course, never did pass.

---

33. *Miss. LJ*, I (1928–29), 46; II (1929–30), 106–07; III (1930–31), 38–39.

Stevens concluded his speech by saying: "Gentlemen of the Bar, if we make any change let it be a longer tenure and a living wage for the judiciary." Five years later at the 1927 meeting members voted to set up a special committee to promote some action by the 1928 Legislature to increase circuit judges' and chancellors' salaries. The members lobbied long, hard, and effectively, and their efforts achieved results. The salaries were raised from $4,000 to $5,000 per year, though with the provision that no incumbent justice or chancellor should receive the raise during his current term.[34]

The members were not only concerned with the condition of the Mississippi judiciary. One of their long standing wishes was met in 1929 when Allen Cox of Baldwyn, after two terms as the first district chancellor, was appointed to be the state's second federal judge serving the northern district. In 1930 they appointed a committee to go to Washington and lobby for Edwin R. Holmes to be appointed to a vacancy that had developed on the bench of the Fifth Circuit Court of Appeals. Not until 1936, however, would Judge Holmes, under a Democratic administration, have the honor of being the first Mississippian to sit on that court.[35]

Looking even further afield, the members in 1929, on a motion by Leroy Percy, voted to urge Mississippi's congressional delegation in Washington to vote for United States membership in the World Court under the terms of the protocol formulated by Elihu Root. But that too would have to wait. President Hoover's administration favored American participation in the Court, but an isolationist filibuster in the Senate in Washington defeated the proposal which, its opponents claimed, had been originated by "international robbers." Meanwhile, at home in Mississippi, members were told at the 1929 meeting that the state Supreme Court, at the suggestion of the Bar Association, on the first day of the September

34. *Miss. Laws* (1928), c. 1.

35. One member of the Mississippi bar, T. G. Bilbo, opposed Holmes' appointment in the U.S. Senate in 1936 [Congressional Record, January–June, 1936, pp. 10081–84], presumably because Holmes in April, 1923, had imprisoned Bilbo for ten days at Oxford for contempt of court. See McLemore, II, 78.

term in 1928 had heard and entered into its permanent records resolutions honoring those members of the state bar who had died during the preceding year. Thus a new custom was established, which, even more than the previously established practice of including memorials in the published proceedings of the Association, must have been a source of comfort and pride to the families of the deceased.

Between the 1929 and 1930 meetings several sessions were held of a special committee of the Association, chaired by Webb Venable, which had been created "to make a survey and study of the administration of justice in the courts of Mississippi." And at Biloxi in 1930 Venable reported their recommendations. They believed that the Association should call on the Legislature to establish by statute a "Judicial Council for the continuous study of the problem of the promotion of justice in our courts." The membership, they suggested, should consist of two Supreme Court justices, two chancellors, two circuit judges, and two county court judges, each pair being elected by their colleagues; and six attorneys, two from each Supreme Court district, three of whom would be chosen by the Association and three by the governor. At their first meeting, the fourteen members thus chosen would then select a fifteenth from among the ranks of the state bar to serve as their chairman. Once established, the Council's function would be to "enact rules governing pleading, practice and procedure in all of our nisi prius courts, such rules to have the force and effect of statutes. . . ." Although the 1930 Legislature had not responded to their call for a permanent commission on law revision, the Association voted to press for creation of this new body in the 1932 legislative session.

A new special committee, headed by V. A. Griffith and including Venable, Dean Kimbrough, Louis C. Hallam, and A. S. Bozeman, was appointed to draft the necessary legislation. But in a report published in the May, 1931, issue of the *Law Journal*, Griffith noted that because of "general adverse conditions which have prevailed throughout the state during the past twelve months, and which are still upon us . . ." the 1932 Legislature would be too busy to consider anything but "questions of State revenues and State finance." Therefore, he said that it would probably be better for his committee to delay making a report until 1932, which would give the Association a further full year to consider their proposals and make any desired changes before they were submitted to the Legislature in 1934. And, indeed, the few members who were present for that 1931 meeting in Meridian, painfully aware that the Association was desperately short of money and already deeply divided over political issues and the question of bar admission standards, were only too glad to postpone consideration of the controversial issue of the Judicial Council till the meeting the following year. Not many of them could have guessed at the time that the "Mississippi State Bar Association," as such, was never to meet again.

IV

The Unification of the Bar

1931–1932

MOST OF THE DISCUSSION in the business sessions at what was destined to be the last annual meeting of the "Mississippi State Bar Association," at Meridian in 1931, had to do with disbarment proceedings then already pending against certain lawyers in the state who had been charged with unethical conduct. Eight years earlier the Standing Committee on Grievances had asked for and received $150 out of the Association's funds in order that they might "employ counsel to take steps towards disbarment of any lawyers of the Mississippi Bar guilty of embezzlement in misappropriating the funds of his client." The bulk of complaints reaching the committee in the 1920s, in fact, had to do with allegations that lawyers had failed to turn over to clients funds collected on their behalf. And in almost every case investigation revealed that a misunderstanding, or at worst an instance of procrastination or minor negligence, had caused the grievance, and matters were soon settled to the satisfaction of all parties concerned.

In 1928, however, committee chairman J. M. Thomas of Tupelo and his two colleagues, George Leftwich of Aberdeen and Victor Gilbert of Meridian, reported that two cases had been referred to them which were of such seriousness that, after consultation with the president and the Executive Committee, they were recommending the appointment by the new president of two special committees to pursue them further. Their recommendation was accepted. A year later, at Clarksdale in 1929, Webb Venable reported that the special committee that he headed had a few weeks earlier been successful in securing the disbarment of one of the accused attorneys in the Boliver County circuit court. Gabe Jacobson reported for the other committee that W. C. Sweat of Corinth had been retained to represent the Association in the second case which concerned a Starkville attorney charged with bigamy and that the disbarment hearing was due to be held in the Oktibbeha chancery court in just a few days' time. In order that the case could be seen through to its conclusion, the members voted to continue the committee.

However, in 1930, in the Assembly Room of the Buena Vista Hotel at Biloxi situated on a pier extending out over the waters of the Gulf, Jacobson informed members that a few weeks earlier Chancellor T. P. Guyton of Kosciusko had announced his decision in favor of the allegedly bigamous attorney because there was no "clear and convincing evidence of his guilt." So the decision was made to discharge the committee. Then the Standing Committee on Grievances got ready to give its report. Before it did so, on a motion by George Leftwich, the Association went into executive session. All non-members, the press, and—to their chagrin—the students from the University law school were required to leave the auditorium.[1]

Everyone knew that some of the cases to be discussed would have to do with the recent highway scandals which already had led to talk of impeachments in the Legislature then still in session in Jackson. In 1928 and 1929 there had been rumors of irregularities and inefficiencies on the part of the elected, eight-man state highway commission set up in 1920. Accordingly Governor Bilbo had gone to the 1930 legislators with a suggestion for a new three-man commission to be appointed by his office. But, instead of accepting that proposal, the lawmakers finally passed the Stansel highway act establishing a three-man elected commission with one commissioner elected from each of the old Supreme Court districts.

1. Hugh Clayton interview (August 17, 1977). Mr. Clayton recalled erroneously that W. L. Guice of Biloxi had called for the non-members to leave. Actually, according to the *Proceedings*, Guice was anxious for all of the accused to be publicly named.

Meanwhile, that spring, as the supporters of each of the two alternative schemes struggled to win majority support, the air had become thick with charges and countercharges of corruption and graft. Most damaging was the allegation by some of the present commissioners that an Ohio firm of roadbuilding contractors, Warren Brothers, had paid out to Carl Marshall, a Bay St. Louis attorney connected with the Bilbo administration, the sum of $80,000 in order to get a $100,000 suit pending against them in the Mississippi courts dropped. Of that $80,000, $62,000 had never been accounted for.

Based on the accusations that had already been made, the committee, headed by Herbert Holmes of Senatobia, recommended that the Association immediately commence disbarment proceedings against Marshall and Jackson lawyer J. H. Howie, both of whom were Association members, as well as three other attorneys whose names had likewise been linked with the Warren Brothers affair. They also recommended that steps be taken to secure the disbarment of a sixth attorney, from Laurel, who was alleged to be guilty of "fraud and deceit in the practice of Law, and the unprofessional practice commonly known as 'ambulance chasing.' " By 63 votes to 15, the members present voted to accept the committee's recommendations and to appoint a new, five-man Special Grievance Committee to initiate disbarment proceedings against the six. Then, on a motion by W. S. Welch and W. L. Guice, it was resolved to proceed against three others whose names had been mentioned in connection with the Warren Brothers case, including Lester C. Franklin, a gubernatorial candidate in 1927 who was presently serving as the State Tax Commissioner.[2]

At the 1931 meeting Jeff Truly of Fayette, chairman of the new Special Grievance Committee, presented a progress report. He and his fellow committee members had first of all resolved that the state Supreme Court, of which he himself had been a member a quarter of a century before, was the proper tribunal in which to conduct statewide disbarment proceedings. So, with the co-opera-

2. *Clarion Ledger*, July 30, 1930, p. 1, col. 7; August 7, 1930, p. 5, col. 3.

tion of the Association's officers, they had gone before that court with the cases referred to them; after mature consideration, the justices had rejected every motion and plea by the defendants against their assuming jurisdiction.[3] Louis M. Jiggitts, "the efficient Secretary" of the Association, had prepared the briefs, and the cases against Marshall, Howie, Franklin, and two of the other defendants were on the docket awaiting trial. The cases against two more were being prepared, and consideration was being given as to what to do about Howie's partner, Sam A. Latham of Jackson, who had left the state. The ambulance chaser had already been disbarred by a lower court, and so no further action would be required with regard to him. Truly recommended, and the members agreed, that his committee continue in being to see the cases through the court. One new case had been referred to them during the past year, that of a Jackson attorney who had been convicted in a Leake County justice of the peace court on a charge of petty larceny for having stolen the sheriff's set of the volumes of the new 1930 *Code*. It was quickly decided that it should be left to the regular Grievance Committee to conduct the further investigation of that case.

Money would obviously be a major problem. The Association's income for 1929–30 had totaled only $1,350, and over $750 had been spent in the previous year's unsuccessful attempt to secure the disbarment of the allegedly bigamous attorney from Starkville. The 1930 Legislature had been asked to appropriate $10,000 to be given to the Association to pay for prosecution of disbarment cases; although the House voted the money, the Senate declined to do so. In 1930–31, the treasurer's report reveals, some of the members had voluntarily contributed a total of $320 to help with the cost of disbarment proceedings, and apparently Truly, Jiggitts, and others had done the necessary work without reimbursement. But, with membership down to a point where the income for annual dues

3. *In Re Steen et al*, *Southern Reporter*, 134:67. The decision had been handed down by the justices sitting *en banc* on April 13, 1931, with only Justice George Ethridge dissenting.

that year was a mere $1,065, the Association as it was then constituted could never hope to carry out properly the task, specifically assigned to it by the Mississippi Code, of enforcing a high standard of legal ethics among the state's lawyers.

Only by bringing in a lot more members could the problem be solved. A decade earlier the Association's leaders had thought that the solution might be to build up a "federated" bar of the type which already existed in Pennsylvania and several other states, deriving its strength from a network of local city and county bar associations affiliated with the state association. Fifteen such groups were already in existence in Mississippi in 1919,[4] and at the annual meeting that year a resolution was passed which "urgently recommended the organization of a local bar association in every county in the State as early as possible. . . ." They were to be modeled along the same lines as the state Association, and to meet every year shortly before the state group's annual meeting to elect their officers. A special committee, with a budget of twenty-five dollars, was set up to work on the project.

But progress was slow. No local associations are listed in the *Proceedings* for the next few years. At the 1923 annual meeting a new tack was tried by amending article V of the Constitution to require the president each year to appoint a vice-president for every county. It would be a county vice-president's job to try to get every lawyer in his county to join the Association. And at the 1927 meeting article IX of the by-laws was amended so as to give him the additional task of working with the Grievance Committee in investigating any complaint lodged against any lawyer or judge residing in his county. The Grievance Committee, for its part, was authorized to co-operate with "a similar committee of any Local or County Bar Association" whenever its members felt it desirable to

4. The *Proceedings* for that year list Adams County, West Point, Hattiesburg, Grenada, Hinds County, Holmes County, Jones County, Oxford, Lauderdale County, Leflore County, Columbus, Pike County, Sunflower County, Warren County, and Washington County. The same fifteen were already in existence in 1917.

do so. At the same time the proposal was made to add a fifteenth article to the Constitution stating that a duly constituted local or county bar association, if a majority of its members voted to do so, could affiliate with the state organization by applying to the Executive Committee. Such an affiliated group would be responsible for paying in annual dues to the secretary-treasurer for all of its members, and no lawyer in a county where there was an association could belong to the state association except through the local group. The last requirement provoked strong opposition from some members, but the new article was approved.

The average American lawyer in that era, however, was inclined to prefer being "a law unto himself, accountable only to God and his conscience,—if any," as Dean Roscoe Pound remarked to a Brooklyn Law School audience in October, 1928. And by 1929 Mississippi still had only eighteen local bar associations, just three more than there had been a decade earlier, according to the A.B.A. annual *Report.*[5] In 1930 and 1931, as we have seen, membership in the state Association declined sharply, and this decline was inevitably accompanied by a corresponding decline in income and effectiveness. Lawyers anyway were not very popular in the Depression, particularly élite lawyers of the type that tended to be most active in the Bar Association. They were the lawyers who represented the big, out-of-state corporations and the banks and who, therefore, usually instituted foreclosure and eviction notices. Consequently, they received severe criticism from outside their ranks at the same time that Governor Bilbo's intervention in the running of the law school, the highway scandal, and disagreement over what policies the Bar should pursue in several vital areas were lowering morale from within.

At the annual meeting in 1931 Jeff Truly was moved to make an impromptu speech. Even though the "Bar of the State of Mississippi," he observed, was undoubtedly the state's "glory in the past: its protection in the present: its hope for the future," there

5. Wickser, pp. 391, 417.

was just then a general tendency, especially among the press, "to malign the Bar as a whole, and to inculcate the idea that disregard of ethics, and dereliction of duty is the general rule of the lawyers of the State applicable to the vast majority thereof." Ten years earlier, Truly had suggested to the annual meeting at Brown's Wells that it should be "made mandatory" for every Mississippi lawyer to belong to the Bar Association. George Butler, in his presidential address at this 1931 meeting, noted: "This association has not exerted as wide an influence or commanded the respect which it should have." He added: "Some means should be derived where each attorney, upon his admission to the bar, should automatically become a member. . . ." The members present, he promised, would hear a proposal for just such a plan from a committee appointed for the purpose.

The voluntary-elective type of association had proved ineffective, and the federated type was obviously impossible. The experience of the 1920s had shown that there was not enough grassroots support among rank and file lawyers in the state to build up such a structure in the only way it could be built, from the bottom upward. So the leadership had become convinced that the only solution was to create in Mississippi what was known as an "incorporated," "unified," or "integrated" state bar.

The concept of an integrated bar had not originated in the populous eastern states, where the practice of law tended to be dominated by the highly-prestigious, organized bar groups in the major metropolitan centers such as Boston, New York, Philadelphia, and Chicago. Instead it had been developed in certain western states where the frontier with its permissive, free-wheeling ways was still a very recent memory, making it difficult for lawyers who believed in such things to try to enforce the high professional standards and the strict code of ethics that were needed if clients' interests were to be protected and lawyers held in high regard. The state bar association of Wisconsin had discussed the idea as early as 1914, the Nebraska bar in 1915, the California bar in 1917; and by 1918 both the A.B.A. and the American Judicature Society had formulated and published a model statute for bar integration.[6] North Dakota was the first state actually to establish an integrated bar by legislative statute in 1921. Alabama and Idaho were second and third in 1923. By 1931 New Mexico, California, Nevada, Oklahoma, South Dakota, and Utah had followed their example. In 1932 it was to be the turn of both Puerto Rico and Mississippi.[7]

The first actual step towards integration had been taken by Dean T. C. Kimbrough. In his presidential address to the 1930 annual meeting at Biloxi, he had expressed his "desire to see the work of the Association more efficient to the end that the profession, the judiciary, and the public may reap a resulting benefit." Nearly every state bar group in the country, he reminded his listeners, had been considerably reorganized during the previous few years in response to a growing realization that merely getting up a yearly convention of friendly fellow professionals was not a good enough justification for their existence. As he saw it, however, Mississippi's organization still "enters into its work with no marked degree of seriousness of purpose" and without any sense of the "necessary objectives to be obtained." Furthermore, because it only involved a small percentage of all of the lawyers in the state, it did not have behind it "the full force of the power of a united bar." His suggestion for dealing with the situation was that they immediately appoint a special committee "of thoughtful and eminent lawyers" and authorize them "to make a careful and comprehensive study" of the issues he had raised. He would particularly recommend for their consideration, he went on to say, "what is known as the inclusive or unified bar plan which has been adopted in several states." He had personally corresponded with the presidents of those state associations and had been told that all of them were

6. Roscoe Pound, *The Lawyer From Antiquity To Modern Times* (St. Paul: West Publishing Co., 1953), p. 272. It has been suggested that proximity to Canada with its unified provincial bars may also have influenced the northwestern states. See *Miss. LJ*, III (1930–31), 322. For the text of the model statute, see *Journal of the American Judicature Society*, II (1918), 111–24.

7. Wickser, pp. 404–05. A.J.S., *Citations*, pp. 1–2; Mississippi's integrated bar statute is wrongly listed as passed in 1930, and Oklahoma (1929) is omitted.

Garvin D. Shands, first president of the Mississippi Bar Association, 1906.

Sydney Smith, president 1914 and 1915 when the constitutional ammendment was passed making the Supreme Court elective rather than appointive. Established State Board of Bar Examiners. He later served on the State Supreme Court and was chief justice for over 20 years.

T. C. Kimbrough, dean of the University of Mississippi Law School when the State Bar was formed in 1935, became president of the Mississippi State Bar in 1929-30.

W. W. Venable, president of the Mississippi State Bar when it was unified in 1932.

John C. Satterfield, president Mississippi State Bar, 1955. President of the American Bar Association in 1959, he has been the only Mississippian to hold this office.

First trustees of the Mississippi Bar Foundation elected in February 1963. They are (left to right): Judge William N. Ethridge, Jr., Hugh N. Clayton, Sidney Carlton, J. K. Dossett, and W. S. Henley. Mr. Henley was the first president of the Foundation. Mr. Carlton was president of the State Bar at that time.

Alice Nevels, executive director of State Bar and first secretary/ treasurer of State Bar Association in 1962-66.

George Van Zant, secretary/treasurer 1966 to present.

Louisiana and Mississippi Bar Association met together for the first time on May 1, 1914 at Gulfport, Mississippi.

Mississippi Bar Association Convention in 1910, held in Vicksburg, Mississippi.

American Bar Association Convention in 1930, held in Biloxi, Mississippi.

State Bar of 1903

"gratified with the results obtained. . . ." There was no undue coercion involved, for not every lawyer had to be an active member. The plan provided for active and non-active members. If it were adopted, he concluded, he looked forward to the day

[w]hen our annual meeting will be regarded as a combination of (1) a company of legal students who are eager to learn from one another and from every available agency; (2) a meeting of stockholders in an important corporation who seek to share the discussion of all its projects; and (3) a fraternity of highminded brethren who are appreciative of the social and friendly intercourse afforded by the Association.

No sooner was Kimbrough seated than Judge D. M. Russell of Gulfport rose to move the appointment of a committee composed of the Dean himself and five others to consider the recommendations that had been made and to report on them at the next annual meeting; he also moved that a preliminary survey of their findings be published in the next issue of the *Law Journal.* W. A. Ellis of Carthage seconded the motion, which was quickly passed.

The committee, appointed by George Butler, the incoming president, was chaired by Kimbrough and also included D. M. Russell, R. E. Wilbourn, D. W. Houston, J. N. Flowers, and W. H. Powell, all of whom, except for Russell, had served terms as president in the past. Their preliminary report eventually appeared in the May, 1931, number of the *Law Journal.*[8] It began with a brief assessment of the twenty-five-year history of the existing Bar Association. It had, they observed, "been able to accomplish good, and has wielded an influence on the whole bar and in the halls of legislation," in spite of being "but loosely knit together, and clothed with no statutory powers." But, for the future, if it was going to "retain the esteem and confidence of the public," it would have to "bring about, through a more efficient organization, those vital things necessary to inspire in the public mind a due and wholesome regard for the profession." Of the two alternative types of

8. III (1930–31), no. 4, 319–29.

bar organizations, they noted that the federated plan had been tried briefly by two states, Oregon and Washington, and then rejected in favor of the unified system; whereas the majority of lawyers in the nine states already using the unified plan seem pleased with it. The Supreme Courts of Idaho, Nevada, and California had all upheld the constitutionality of their integrated bar acts. Finally, an integrated bar, the committee members felt, would give Mississippi lawyers "adequate machinery for dealing with such questions as professional ethics, discipline, unlawful practice of the law, educational requirements, distribution of information, public relations and research in problems of legislative and judicial reform." It was their recommendation that the Association's president for 1931–32 be authorized to appoint a committee of five members, one from each Supreme Court district and two from the state at large, to draft the necessary legislation for an incorporated bar act that would be in compliance with the state's constitution and then bring it to the 1932 annual meeting for approval.

Since many members had probably not yet had time to read the committee's report before leaving their homes to attend the 1931 meeting at Meridian, the *Law Journal's* editor-in-chief, Hugh N. Clayton, went around on the opening day, April 29, handing out extra copies. At an informal gathering held the previous evening in the hotel, both the pros and cons of the proposals had been the subject of vigorous discussion. A majority of the lawyers present, it turned out, were prepared not only to accept them but to press ahead with them even faster than the committee had anticipated. The first action taken at the business meeting on the 29th was to delete the final section of the report calling for a new committee to report in 1932. A proposed second amendment, to the effect that no lawyer should be required to join a unified bar against his will, was tabled; then a motion to adopt the report as amended was carried. Next it was resolved that a draft statute be composed by the committee and submitted to the members the following day.

President Butler appointed W. W. Venable, A. T. Stovall, and

W. H. Watkins to work with R. E. Wilbourn and J. N. Flowers in drawing up the bill. On the morning of April 30, however, their chairman, Flowers, asked for more time to complete the task assigned them. He proposed that he and his associates prepare a draft bill to be published in the next number of the *Law Journal.* Members should then have thirty days to communicate their "suggestions and criticisms" to him in Jackson before the final version was submitted to the Executive Committee for its approval. Then, if approved, a specially appointed steering committee would take it to the Legislature. Motions to accept Flowers' proposals and to authorize the incoming president to appoint the steering committee were carried unanimously after only brief discussions.

In fact Flowers' committee did not get its report in to President Venable until September 2, 1931, too late for the autumn issue of the *Journal.* But it was printed in the February, 1932, issue, together with the full text of the proposed act which was already by then being considered by the Legislature.[9]

Although a legal historian has written that "for the first ten or fifteen years integration was accomplished under the model form of statute" proposed by the American Judicature Society,[10] the "proposed Bar Unification Act" for Mississippi bore little resemblance to the A.J.S. draft. Flowers observed that their version was "analogous, in a general way, to measures adopted in other states." It most nearly resembled the one already in effect in Alabama but was different in at least two important essentials: it did not give the State Association the power to control admissions to the bar, and it did not confer on them the final authority to suspend or disbar attorneys.[11] A close comparison shows very few similarities to the model statute. Besides the two important differences already mentioned, the Mississippi Bar was to be governed by a president, first vice-president, second vice-president, and a board of commis-

9. IV (1931–32), 205–15.

10. George E. Brand, "Bar Organization and Judicial Administration—A New Horizon," *Journal of the American Judicature Society*, XXXIV (1950), no. 2, 40.

11. Cf. the model statute, secs. 29 and 31.

sioners elected from each one of the circuit court districts for one-year terms; whereas the model statute called for a president and vice-president and fifteen "governors" serving for staggered five-year terms. The Mississippi version, said President Venable, was "the result of careful study by an able committee." He called on all of the state's lawyers to support it by lobbying their local legislative representatives for its speedy passage.

The newly elected Legislature which convened in Jackson in the first week of January, 1932, was primarily concerned with the ruined financial condition of the state, a situation that mirrored all too accurately the poverty-stricken condition of so many of its citizens. They discovered that they had inherited over fifty million dollars worth of debts. Merchants were no longer willing to extend credit to state institutions, and teachers and other employees were being paid with certificates which could only be cashed at a twenty percent discount. The new governor, Martin Sennett Connor, offered as his solution the "Emergency Revenue Act" which would institute a three percent sales tax. The heated, and sometimes even violent, controversy that his proposal provoked (and after March 1 a spate of sensational stories concerning the Lindbergh baby kidnapping) meant that the press had little attention to spare for the progress of the integrated bar bill.[12] On April 12, however, it was reported that both houses had approved a final version of the bill worked out by a conference committee. A week later, on April 19th, the same day that the Legislature finally approved a two percent sales tax by a single vote in the House of Representatives, Governor Connor signed the "unified bar act" into law.[13]

The wording of the "Act to provide for the organization, regulation and government of the Mississippi State Bar, to require all lawyers now or hereafter practicing law within this state to become members of the association . . . and to define the powers and duties of such association" differs very little in most respects from

12. McLemore, II, 97–99, 102–03. *Clarion Ledger*, March 1–April 12, 1932, *passim*.

13. *Clarion Ledger*, April 13, 1932, p. 7, col. 6; April 20, 1932, passim. *Miss. Laws* (1932), c. 121.

the version originally drawn up by Flowers' committee. The first fourteen sections are exactly identical. Section 15 was expanded to include both "the judges of the federal courts" and "persons having practiced less than one year" in the categories of those who could be members without having to pay dues. All of the other changes were made in sections 23 to 29, dealing with the investigation of alleged misconduct by an attorney and the conduct of disbarment or reinstatement proceedings. The last half of section 23, part 2, which would have given the Board of Commissioners, "subject to the approval of the justices of the supreme court," the power to formulate the procedural rules for handling reinstatement applications and to make recommendations to the Supreme Court concerning them, was deleted. The proposed section 25, which stated that nothing in the statute should be understood as altering any existing legislation or court regulations concerning misconduct by attorneys but rather as supplementing them and that the Association would have "no jurisdiction of complaints based upon acts done or committed" prior to its enactment, was cut out entirely. In the proposed section 26, renumbered as 25, the sentence was taken out which would have specifically authorized court officials to end the suspension of a delinquent who had paid up his back dues without waiting to receive official notice that he had done so from the Association secretary. Instead the precise timing of a reinstatement was left, perhaps deliberately, rather vague.

The most drastic changes were made in the proposed section 27, renumbered as 26, the main section dealing with disbarments. Rather sensibly the stipulation that the Commissioners should investigate, with a view to disbarment, any complaint that an attorney had been guilty "of a violation of the criminal laws of the state" was cut out. Even the most upright of jurists might be unfortunate enough to get a ticket for jaywalking, and a good many members of the bar seem to have been in the habit of breaking the liquor laws on a regular basis. But the main thrust of the changes was to take out of the hands of the Supreme Court justices the power directly to regulate disbarment procedures and to make all disbarment judgments themselves without the need for a previous hearing before a circuit judge or chancellor. The requirement that the Association's rules of professional conduct were to be promulgated "with the approval of the justices of the Supreme Court" was also deleted. Most of the rest of the section was entirely rewritten so as to include a set of requirements that were briefly repeated and summarized in the new section 27 which read: "The Circuit or Chancery Court of the county in which the party whose interest is involved resides, shall have exclusive original jurisdiction in all matters pertaining to disbarment, but either party may appeal to the Supreme Court." The legislators in fact seem to have been unwilling to entrust disbarments entirely to such an élite group of lawyers as the Bar Commissioners or to the élite group of judges who sat on the bench of the state's highest court. An attorney accused of malfeasance was to be tried, initially at least, among his neighbors in a court in which he himself was accustomed to practice.

The unification measure, bill number 281, had been brought on to the floor of the House of Representatives on February 12 with the backing of forty-two sponsors, of which thirty-two were practicing lawyers and six were law students attending the University of Mississippi Law School. Of the lawyer-sponsors the names of only five appear on the list of active Bar Association members for 1931–32: J. A. Lake and S. V. Anderson of Greenville, Thompson McClellan of West Point, P. M. Stockett of Woodville, and Walter Sillers of Rosedale. Among the six students were Jamie L. Whitten, the future U.S. Congressman, and J. M. Ewing, the future president of Delta State University. Another lawyer-sponsor was Mrs. Joseph Howorth, formerly Lucy Somerville, who had followed in her mother's footsteps by winning election to the Legislature.

House action on the bill was rapid. It was sent immediately to the Judiciary Committee chaired by Walter Sillers, who was already by then a very influential member of the House over which he was destined to preside as Speaker from 1944 to 1966. Three days later Sillers reported it out with the recommendation that it be passed as written, and on the following day, the 16th, he successfully moved to suspend the rules so that it could be given its third and final reading and be voted on right away. The vote was favorable by 105 to 5. Only one of the five nays, George Robert Smith of Pass Christian, was a lawyer; the other four presumably voted in the negative at the behest of lawyer friends opposed to the measure. The following day a motion by H. E. Mason, a non-lawyer from Wayne County, to reconsider the bill was quickly tabled, and it went up to the Senate.[14]

Things in the upper house did not go so quickly. Not until a month later, on March 17, did W. A. Blair, the Tupelo lawyer who served as chairman of the Senate's Judiciary Committee, report out the bill and recommend its passage as amended. By that stage he and his committee had already made most of the changes described above in the text of the original draft. On March 28, when it came up for a vote by the full Senate, Senator T. M. McIntosh, a lawyer from Collins, offered an amendment from the floor to lower the annual dues payable to the unified bar to $2.50. He had few backers for his proposal, however, and the amended bill was approved by 20 votes to 7 with 22 abstentions. That might have done it, but in the House a week later, on April 5, Sillers won majority backing for a motion not to accept the Senate's amendments. And that was why a conference had to be held between the two houses in order to try to effect a compromise. Sillers, Bradford Dye, and J. S. Butler, a non-lawyer sponsor of the bill, were chosen to represent the lower house on the conference committee, while, in addition to Blair, the upper house was represented by W. B. Roberts of Rosedale, and D. C. Bramlette of Woodville. The last two were lawyers and, unlike Blair, members of the existing Association. As it turned out, only a few changes were made by the conference in the Senate's amended version. The Board of Commissioners itself was empowered to reprimand an attorney for an offense that was not deemed serious enough to warrant disbarment, and the Supreme Court, in hearing disbarment or reinstatement appeals, was

14. *House Journal* (1932), pp. 252, 263, 268, 271, 550. For an account of Walter Sillers' political career, see T. R. Melton, "Mr. Speaker: A Biography of Walter Sillers" (unpublished M.A. thesis, University of Mississippi, 1972).

empowered, in such matters only, to render judgment on the facts of the case and not just on matters of law. The House of Representatives, on April 12, voted to approve the conference committee's revised version of the bill by 91 votes to 24 with 29 absent or abstaining. The vote in the Senate was 31 for, none against, and 18 absent or abstaining. So in both houses ultimately an overall majority of the members cast their votes for an integrated bar.[15]

The June issue of the *Journal of the American Judicature Society* announced the news to lawyers across America: "Mississippi Bar Unified by Statute." After noting that it was the tenth integrated bar act to be passed in the United States and that it was based on the Alabama act of 1923, the *Journal* observed that the main difference was that the Mississippi State Bar had not been given control over admissions to the profession. Section 15, with its provision that state and federal judges could become members with an option as to whether or not they paid annual dues, was especially praised as "an ingenious and satisfactory way of dealing with lawyers in judicial office."[16]

Another good aspect of the new legislation, noted by the *Journal*, was that it provided "a convenient way of getting the State Bar organized." Sections 4 and 5 stipulated the procedures to be followed. Within 30 days of the act being signed into law by the governor, each circuit judge was required to appoint a lawyer resident in his district, who was in good standing, to serve on the first Board of Commissioners. Then it was up to the secretary of state, in not less than ten nor more than twenty-one days after the thirty days were up, to call those appointed to an organizational meeting in his office.

Secretary of State Walker Wood in fact wasted little time. The prescribed meeting was held on May 30, just forty-four days after the integrated bar act had become law. Those present were Ben H. McFarland of Aberdeen (from the first district), John L. Heiss of

---

15. *House Journal* (1932), *passim. Senate Journal* (1932), pp. 641–42, 669–70 and *passim. Miss. Code Annotated* (1942), 6A recompiled, title 32, chap. 2, div. 2, secs. 8685–8724, pp. 228–40.

16. XVI (1932), no. 1, p. 7.

Gulfport (second), Fred B. Smith of Ripley (third), Frank E. Everett of Indianola (fourth), John D. Guyton of Kosciusko (fifth), Representative David C. Bramlette of Woodville (sixth), Louis M. Jiggitts of Jackson (seventh), C. E. Johnson of Union (eighth), R. M. Kelly of Vicksburg (ninth), C. C. Dunn of Meridian (tenth), W. W. Venable of Clarksdale (eleventh), George W. Currie of Hattiesburg (twelfth), W. D. Hilton of Mendenhall (thirteenth), J. H. Price of Magnolia (fourteenth), Lee D. Hall of Columbia (fifteenth), W. G. Roberds of West Point (sixteenth), and John Kyle of Sardis (seventeenth).[17]

Their first actions were to choose W. W. Venable, the incumbent president of the existing Bar Association, to chair the meeting and then immediately afterwards to elect him by acclamation president of the newly instituted State Bar. A native of Clinton, Venable had begun his law career at Meridian. After serving for six years as district attorney and for two years as judge for the tenth circuit, in 1916 he had been elected to the United States House of Representatives from the fifth congressional district in the face of strong opposition from the Vardaman forces. By 1922, his congressional career ended, he was settled in Clarksdale, practicing law once again and serving as city attorney.

R. L. Dent of Collins, the incumbent vice-president, though he was not one of the appointed Commissioners, was elected first vice-president of the new State Bar and J. H. Price was elected second vice-president, again both of them by acclamation. With the same unanimous approval Jiggitts was picked to continue as secretary-treasurer. President Venable's first official act was to appoint Smith, Heiss, and Dunn as a committee to draw up a list of proposed by-laws for presentation to the annual general meeting. Arrangements were made with Secretary of State Wood for Jiggitts to be allocated office space in the Capitol building as required by section 10 of the act, and to comply with section 8 it was decided that he should take the necessary steps to have himself bonded to the

17. Commissioners' Minutes for May 30, 1932. Three of the nominated Commissioners would later serve terms on the Mississippi Supreme Court: Hall (1949–61), Kyle (1950–65), and Roberds (1940–60).

amount of $3,000. The morning's business ended with a report on the status of the disbarment proceedings against those attorneys implicated in the Warren Brothers road-paving scandal. Sitting *en banc* on November 30, 1931, the justices of the Supreme Court had unanimously acquitted J. H. Howie and, because they were evenly divided, three to three, over his case, had also dismissed the petition against Lester C. Franklin; however, at the same time they had disbarred Carl Marshall and another attorney named Steen. On February 1, 1932, they had also disbarred Howie's partner, Sam A. Latham, who had never returned from Illinois.[18] Marshall now was getting ready to sue for reinstatement in the chancery court of Hancock County, and, at Venable's request, the Commissioners heard a brief report from one of his lawyers, Bidwell Adam of Pass Christian, who had served as lieutenant-governor in the recently concluded Bilbo administration (1928–32).

When the Commissioners reconvened after lunch, it was decided to have the president appoint two further committees: one to study general questions of concern to the Bar and another to compile a draft code of canons and ethics. Before they finally adjourned, Venable was accorded a standing ovation "for the work done by him in behalf of the passage of the new bar act," and he was asked to pick a date for a general meeting of the members to be held also in the Capitol in accordance with the act's section 35. The commissioners themselves would assemble again in Jackson the day before the meeting was due to begin in order to be certain that everything was ready.[19]

Three months later, on September 1, 1932, some 475 lawyers gathered at 10:00 A.M. in Jackson's Robert E. Lee Hotel for what was billed as the "First Annual Meeting of the Mississippi State Bar." After the opening formalities were concluded, the president of the American Bar Association, Guy A. Thompson of Missouri, gave the annual address very appropriately taking as his topic,

---

18. For the November 30, 1931, disbarment decisions, see *Southern Reporter*, 138:297–329. For Latham's case, see *Mississippi Reports*, 162:233–37.
19. Commissioners' Minutes.

"The Organized Bar." Although the Great Depression, he observed, was hard on everyone, lawyers were coming in for more than their fair share of the blame. Their only adequate defense was to maintain, and insist on, their traditionally high standards of professional responsibility:

> . . . in these modern days, in the firmament of our profession, above the weathered mists and dark clouds of depression—almost desperation, almost despair—shines our Star of Duty—duty to client, duty to profession, duty to country. Let us fix our eyes upon that Star and with upturned faces bathed in its effulgent glory, like the Wise Men of old, let us follow it.

The members responded with "Continued Applause."

Then, Venable, in his presidential address, discussed "the purpose of the law which forms us into a statewide and all inclusive legal society." The Bar had asked for and had been given, he said, "the task of improving the conditions for justice under law." The people of Mississippi, through their legislators, had "expressed a confidence that with our new and official status and with our forces combined, we can render a better public service." They were empowered, he reminded them, "to investigate and study anything pertaining to law and courts and to make our studied recommendations to the legislature when legislation is needed." He then went on to suggest several topics that might repay study, including major reforms in the organization and procedures of the state's courts, a program for systematically annotating the A.L.I.'s Restatements as they came out, and methods of enforcing high ethical standards among lawyers. None of these meant, he concluded, that the organized bar should not also be a vehicle for good fun and good fellowship among members of what was, after all, a professional "great brotherhood."

After some discussion the set of by-laws, consisting of eleven articles composed by the Commissioners' committee, was approved as written. The draft code of ethics was speedily approved also, but only after canon 39, which would have required a lawyer to disclose in court any fees or other compensation paid to one of his witnesses in excess of the statutory allowances, was deleted and the subsequent canons renumbered. The Commissioners' suggested budget, reported by Secretary Jiggitts, was based on the assumption that there were 1300 lawyers in the state, actually somewhat of an underestimate, and that at least 1100 of them would pay the $5 annual dues. So $5,500 was assumed to be the total available to work with, some two and a half times the average for the preceding decade. The stenographer employed to assist in the Carl Marshall disbarment case was still owed $600 for his work, and Jiggitts' own salary, because of the extra work involved in handling a much larger membership, was to be raised from $300 to $675 a year. The only item disallowed by the members was $200 to pay contributors of articles to the *Law Journal*. They would have to be content with the honor only.

Leslie Darden of Hernando, editor-in-chief of the *Journal*, who was present at the meeting, was probably not too disturbed by the cut, for the members did approve $1,000 for the general support of the publication, more than had ever been allotted before. Also pleased no doubt was T. C. Kimbrough who had been restored to the deanship of the University law school a few weeks earlier. The outgoing dean, Bilbo's appointee Stone Deavours, gave "a very fine talk" at the final session on the afternoon of the second day on the "History of the Ole Miss Law School." "Much interest was shown" in what he had to say, but no record of his address was ever published.[20] Then, as the *Clarion Ledger* had predicted even before the meeting began, the members proceeded to elect "Judge Jeff Truly of Fayette, statewide known because of his participation in the Carl Marshall disbarment trial" and the one who eleven years earlier had been the first to call for a bar organization to which all lawyers in the state belonged, as the first full term president of the newly unified Mississippi State Bar.[21]

20. According to the *Clarion Ledger*, September 3, 1932, p. 1, col. 6, his subject was "legal ethics," so perhaps he stressed that aspect of the school's curriculum.

21. *Clarion Ledger*, September 1, 1932, p. 14, col. 6, September 3, 1932, p. 1, cols. 6–7.

V

The Early History of the Unified Bar

1932–1952

As things turned out, the Carl Marshall case was to be President Truly's main concern during his first seven months in office, and the way it was finally decided must have been a source of great frustration to him. On September 2, 1932, the very same day the elderly judge from Fayette was elected to head the State Bar, and, while Marshall was himself in Jackson soliciting support from old friends and colleagues, Chancellor D. M. Russell in the Harrison County Chancery Court, in accordance with the terms of the unified bar act, decreed that the Bay St. Louis attorney was to be reinstated as a practicing lawyer as of October 2. In an accompanying statement Chancellor Russell acknowledged that the State Bar had challenged his jurisdiction in the case because Marshall had been disbarred by the Supreme Court before the bar act had become law and that many people thought an attorney who "had shown no penitence nor so much as admitted that he had been guilty of 'blackmail and perjury' " had no right to ask for reinstatement only a few months after being disbarred. For these reasons he had taken more than two months to reach his decision, and he fully realized that the leaders of the bar would probably appeal it. Since the new act allowed up to sixty days for such an appeal, the *Clarion Ledger* observed, Marshall actually had little hope of returning to practice in less than a year from the date of his disbarment in November, 1931.[1]

Seventeen months had elapsed, in fact, when the Supreme

1. September 3, 1932, p. 1, col. 1; p. 7, col. 2.

Court reaffirmed the Chancellor's decree reinstating Marshall on April 17, 1933. In the meantime, apparently most of his fellow lawyers in his own home district had come to feel a great deal of pity for the young attorney. According to his own testimony, he had spent seven weeks in the hospital recovering from a nervous breakdown brought on by his troubles. Barred from practicing his profession, and with a family to support, he was very nearly destitute. Perhaps his colleagues considered that he had been made the "fall guy" by other more guilty, but also more powerful, men. In the autumn of 1932 the Harrison County Bar Association passed a resolution endorsing his petition for reinstatement, and five prominent barristers from the Coast had joined with former lieutenant governor Adam, former governor Earl Brewer (1912–1916), and Charles Engle of Natchez as his attorneys of record.

Brewer, Engle, and two Gulfport lawyers, J. A. Leathers and J. L. Taylor, were the ones who actually pleaded Marshall's case before the Supreme Court. The appellants' case was argued on behalf of the State Bar Commissioners by Venable and J. H. Price, who had also opposed Marshall's reinstatement before Chancellor Russell. Marshall's victory, when it came, was achieved by the narrowest of margins. Three of the six high court justices were opposed to readmitting him: J. G. McGowen, W. D. Anderson, and Chief Justice Smith, who stated in his dissenting opinion that the reinstatement was "calculated to, and [might] shake public confidence in the courts and in the integrity of the legal profession." The three other justices, however, G. H. Ethridge, V. A. Griffith, and W. H. Cook were all in agreement that since his disbarment Marshall had lived "an exemplary life" and had "rehabilitated himself, and is now worthy of being reinstated." The three to three tie meant that the lower court's judgment was upheld.[2]

Judge Truly saved his public comments on the outcome of the

---

2. *Southern Reporter*, 147:791–807, *Mississippi Reports*, 165:538–82. *Clarion Ledger*, April 18, 1933, p. 2, col. 2. Marshall's other attorneys of record before the Supreme Court were S. C. Mize and B. E. Eaton of Gulfport, and W. L. Guice of Biloxi.

appeal for his presidential address at the 1933 meeting in Vicksburg. He deplored the situation whereby a

> banished lawyer after a few months of cessation of practice can appear before the judge of his own choosing, accompanied by his own friends, and there, by protesting sorrow and a desire for rehabilitation and a promise of future observance of the ethical tenets which he has once violated, must again be admitted to the professional brotherhood which cast him out. And that too without confession of guilt, without returning the fruits of offence.

"If that be the law," he said, "and so it remain, then the efforts of the Bar to elevate its standard of ethics, to forestall the justice of criticism, to be shielded against the shafts of calumny, all are unavailing." He called for new legislation whereby either reinstatements must be approved by the State Bar, with appeal from their decision to the Supreme Court, or else the Supreme Court be restructured so that a tie decision could no longer have the same momentous result. But no such legislation was enacted; many of the members at Vicksburg may have felt that Marshall had suffered enough.

The proceedings of the 1933 meeting published in the *Law Journal* referred to it as "the twenty-eighth annual meeting of the Mississippi State Bar." That was thanks to A. T. Stovall who, pointing out that the A.B.A. still numbered its meetings from the first informal gathering at Saratoga Springs in 1878 and not from the date of its formal incorporation, had moved successfully to resume the numbering from 1906. By voting to do so, the members recognized that there had been a very real continuity from the old Bar Association to the new State Bar particularly with regard to the succession of officers and the leadership generally.

Presidents Venable, Truly, and J. H. Price (1933–34) ensured that a smooth transition took place, ably assisted by Louis M. Jiggitts, last secretary of the old, and first secretary of the new, organization. In 1929 Jiggitts had been appointed Supreme Court reporter and probably soon found that he could not do that job properly and also continue to handle the day to day affairs of a bar group that had tripled in size. In 1933 he stood down and was replaced as secretary-treasurer by Walter W. Capers. Capers resigned in 1935 and was replaced by Mrs. Alice Nevels, the first non-lawyer to hold the position, who made it her fulltime job.

Jiggitts, Capers, and Nevels served the needs of a Bar membership that expanded from about 1400 to about 1500 during the decade of the thirties; some 250 to 300 of the members attended the annual meetings. Presumably because nearly everyone was suffering from the effects of the Depression, and in order to make the meetings inexpensively accessible to a majority of those members wishing to attend, cities located in the south-central or central areas of the state were always picked as meeting places prior to 1939. After Vicksburg in 1933 the Bar visited Hattiesburg in 1934, Natchez in 1935, Greenville in 1936, Meridian in 1937, and Vicksburg again in 1938. Vicksburg was probably attractive, among other obvious reasons, because after the end of federal prohibition in 1933 alcoholic beverages were readily available there. They were easily obtained in Biloxi and Gulfport also, but the members seem to have wanted to avoid the comparatively expensive Coast resorts. Still there were complaints in 1935 that the customary registration fee of three to five dollars was too high for a man who brought his family with him; it was suggested that the Bar pay all the costs of the annual banquet as it had done prior to 1932, but the suggestion was not considered.

Whatever the cost there was always a wide variety of entertainment planned for members and their guests by the local bar. At Natchez in 1935 there was a square dance at five-thirty on the first night, September 6, in the Eola Hotel, followed by a formal ball at nine. The annual banquet was held on the second night also at the Eola. Meanwhile other activities included a "picture show," a pilgrimage, and a horseshoe pitching contest. Though the schedules varied from year to year, the emphasis was always on dancing one night and on dining the other. At Meridian in 1937 there was a reception for the ladies at the country club at four on the first afternoon, followed by an outdoor barbecue for everyone at six, and a reception and dance at nine. Again the annual banquet was held the second night.

The outdoor activities were probably included in the Meridian program due to the fact that the meeting was held on June 17th and 18th instead of in mid-September. The year before, at Greenville, members had expressed a general desire to amend article V of the by-laws so as to return to having meetings in the spring. April was not ideal because the federal and some state courts would still be in session, and May was rejected because the University would still be operating and the law students, busy getting ready for final exams, would be discouraged from attending. So mid-June was chosen and has continued to be the time for the annual meeting ever since. Another change was made in 1938 when the Commissioners decided to have the meeting in Vicksburg last for three days as had been the practice from 1907 to 1914, but with nothing planned for the last night. Unification of the bar had meant that more people came and wanted to speak; so it was probably felt that the expanded schedule would make for more effective sessions. But a serious disadvantage was soon apparent. Many members decided to start back home before the final business session on the third afternoon when the new officers were elected and the site for the following year's meeting picked. That very first year in Vicksburg, although 282 members had registered the first day, only thirty were present for those final important votes.

That fact, plus the general improvement in the economy of the state at the end of the decade, probably explains how the decision came to be made to return at long last to the Gulf Coast by choosing Biloxi as host city for the 1939 Bar meeting. Jackson was visited in 1940 for the first time in eight years. In 1941 there was a return to the Coast at Gulfport, but for two days only. Thereafter, except for a final visit to Meridian in 1943 and in 1948 when the Bar met on the campus of the University of Mississippi which was celebrating its 100th anniversary, meetings were always held at Gulfport, Biloxi, or Jackson.

Beginning with the Jackson meeting in 1940 the *Law Journal*, perhaps because the war, already underway in Europe, had made paper scarce and expensive, stopped publishing a complete stenographic record of the annual meetings, which is unfortunate for the historian. Seven years earlier history had been made when WPFB in Hattiesburg broadcast the major speeches from the 1934 meeting there. At the same meeting the members voted to create a Committee on the History of the Bar. The following year, at Natchez, the committee members in their report recommended the creation of a "History Section" of the Mississippi State Bar whose primary function would be "the preservation and publication of the legal history of the State of Mississippi." Other recommendations made by the committee, which was chaired by Judge J. Morgan Stevens, were that municipal and county officials around the state should be encouraged to deposit their old records with the State Archives for safekeeping and that the Legislature be urged to provide the Archives Department with a suitable building to house their collections. The headquarters of the Bar's History Section, it was suggested, should be in the same building.

Their recommendations were accepted by the members with enthusiasm, but after that no more is heard of the History Section. Perhaps the reason was that Dr. Dunbar Rowland, director of the state's Department of Archives and History and a member of the Jackson bar, who had served on the committee and probably had been its main driving force, died in 1937 just two years after the publication of volume I of his classic work, *Courts, Judges, and Lawyers of Mississippi.*[3]

The lawyers, judges, and courts of Mississippi were of course always the principal concern of the State Bar. In 1933 and 1934, however, national politics intruded to some extent into the annual meetings. The annual address in the former year was given by Mississippi's United States Senator Pat Harrison who spoke on behalf of the legislative proposals of the newly-inaugurated Democratic administration headed by Franklin Delano Roosevelt. Afterwards the members voted unanimously that they were "in full accord with the President's efforts to bring [the] country out of its

3. Jackson: State Department of Archives and History, 1935.

present chaotic condition," and that a telegram be sent to the White House stating "that the Members of the Mississippi State Bar are in full accord with your National Recovery Act." Then H. B. Greaves of Canton made a motion that the governor be asked to take the necessary steps to give Mississippians a chance to vote on the proposed Twenty-first Amendment to the U.S. Constitution which was to repeal the Eighteenth (prohibition) Amendment. "That is a part of the National Democratic Platform," he observed, "and we are committed to it." But Charles Garnett of Columbus objected. "Are we not approaching upon politics in this matter?" he asked, "and should we not keep clear of getting into the maelstrom of partisanship?" Most members agreed that they should, and the motion was tabled.

By 1934 some loss of enthusiasm for the new regime in Washington was evident among the members. Speaking on "Recent Federal Legislation," Barney Eaton of Gulfport complained: "The troublous times are not only producing financial distress; they are producing confusion of thought and dangerous governmental experimentation." After that year, divisive political issues ceased to be discussed, formally at least, at Bar meetings.

Senator Harrison, in fact, was the only major political celebrity invited to address an annual meeting during the 1930s. In 1934 Nathan P. Bryant, presiding judge of the Fifth Circuit Court of Appeals, spoke on the mission of a state bar association. In 1935 Dean Leon Green of the Northwestern University law school discussed "the administrative process" and two years later Herschel W. Arant, Dean of the law school at Ohio State University, argued in favor of stricter standards for admission to the bar. In 1936 Lamar Hardy, a native of Pass Christian, talked of the problems that he had trying to enforce the law in his capacity as district attorney in the southern district of New York. And in 1939 a nonlawyer, Frank R. Ahlgren, executive editor of the Memphis *Commercial Appeal*, discussed "the lawyer, the people and the press."

The year before that an element of New Deal politics had been reintroduced into the proceedings by Assistant U.S. Attorney General Joseph B. Keenan when he spoke on "the dynastic power of big business." What he said provoked little response, but it may have reminded some members of a report given by John Brunini of Vicksburg for the Committee on Attorneys' Fees at the 1935 meeting. "For the last two years," he said, "it has been apparent to some of us that some of the liability and casualty companies are undertaking to recoup the losses they have sustained in their investment departments by reducing the cost of operation in other departments." Some companies were, in fact, demanding that the attorneys they retained provide a detailed accounting of the hours spent working for them. The committee's recommendation, which was approved, was that a permanent committee of the State Bar be created to pass upon any complaints concerning fees from either attorneys or the companies that hired their services.

The organization of the new unified Bar included no permanent standing committees. Instead committees were appointed on an *ad hoc* basis as they were needed, by the Commissioners. There always had to be a *Law Journal* committee, however, and those who served on it did a good job during the 30's. In 1933 committee chairman, Frank E. Everett of Indianola persuaded the members to restore to the *Journal's* budget the $200 that had been cut the previous year as unnecessary to attract articles. In 1934 the subsidy was raised to $1,500, and by 1939–40 the State Bar was subsidizing the publication to the tune of $2,000, approximately one-third of the Bar's total budget.[4] Perhaps the fact that from 1936 on it was printed in Mississippi rather than in Jackson, Tennessee, contributed to their willingness to do so.

The University Law School, which had the responsibility for publishing the *Journal*, also continued to enjoy the strong support of the Bar. By the time of the 1933 meeting, with T. C. Kimbrough back as dean and its accreditation by the A.A.L.S. restored, the school was entering upon a new era of both tranquillity and excellence. Dean Kimbrough, Frank Everett told members that year, "has got a 'darned' good law school up at Oxford." But not every would-be lawyer could afford to spend three years studying law at

4. According to the annual financial report published in the *Law Journal*, the Bar's total expenditure in 1939–40 was $6,202.99.

the University. In October, 1930, therefore, two Jackson lawyers, Walter W. Capers and L. J. Calhoun, in partnership with William Hemingway and John H. Fox, Jr., two professors forced to leave the University temporarily by Governor Bilbo, had founded the Jackson School of Law in order "to provide instruction in evening classes [and] to offer an opportunity to study law to those who must earn their livelihood while participating in study." Although it was a private, commercial enterprise, the school held its classes on the campus of Millsaps College and so perhaps had some claim to be recognized as the successor to the old Millsaps College Law School which had gone out of existence in 1918.[5]

But nearly half of the state's lawyers continued to receive their training at "Ole Miss,"[6] and the welfare of the University's school of law continued to be an important concern of the State Bar. At the 1939 meeting a resolution was passed noting with alarm the fact that "the professors in our Law School, in which the Bar is greatly interested, are very much underpaid; . . . they are being paid less salaries [*sic*] than in any other State supported law school in the United States." A committee of five was set up to try to persuade Chancellor Butts, the Board of Trustees, and, if necessary, the Legislature to do something about it. The Legislature did not increase the University's appropriation in 1940;[7] nevertheless, Dean Kimbrough reported proudly at the annual meeting that year on the work the law school was doing and the practical curriculum it offered.

In addition to their practical courses, the dean emphasized, the law students were also still required to take a course in legal ethics. Most members of the State Bar firmly believed that sound legal ethics were just as important as sound legal training. Under the constitution of the unified Bar one of the seventeen Commissioners each year was designated to be the "Complaint Commissioner." His job was to consider all complaints of mispractice or unprofessional conduct made against Mississippi lawyers and to draw the attention of his fellow commissioners to any case that might contain

5. McLemore, II, 381–82.
6. *Miss. LJ*, XIII (1940–41), 714.
7. *Miss. Laws* (1938), c. 20; *ibid.* (1940), c. 6.

grounds for a reprimand, a suspension, or perhaps an action for disbarment. The occasional reports appearing in the published accounts of the annual meetings indicate that around thirty complaints were received each year, the great majority of which, as had been the case in the past, were due to some oversight or misunderstanding on the part of either the attorney involved or the complainant. Fewer than ten percent led to the initiation of a disbarment, and none caused the stir that the Carl Marshall case had.

One large category of lawyers in the state who might all have been suspended if section 25 of the Unified Bar Act had been rigorously enforced was the approximately one-tenth who regularly failed to pay the annual dues of $5. Section 25 stated that, after two months' written notice of his delinquency, any attorney "shall thereby stand suspended from membership in the Mississippi State Bar." The secretary was supposed to inform the courts in the delinquent's district of his suspension, and he was not to be readmitted to practice until all the dues in arrears were paid. But, just as in the old voluntary Bar Association, non-payment of dues seems never to have led to the member's being expelled as called for in the by-laws, so in the 1930s and 1940s the full rigor of the law seems never to have been applied to the non-payers.

At the annual meeting for 1933, it had been noted by President Truly that some members of the Bar were at first opposed to the new organization because they disliked the compulsory aspect and feared that the duties of membership would prove too onerous. But the courts had upheld the Unified Bar's legality, and "after twelve months of operation practical unanimity of thought and action [had] been reached throughout the entire legal fraternity of this state." Nevertheless, by 1935 the number of non-payers was at the ten percent level. By 1938 there were 142 out of 1193 active members of the bar (thirteen and a half percent) who owed a total of $2,020 in back dues. Fifteen of them had never paid any dues. Publishing the names of the delinquents in the *Law Journal* from 1936 on made no difference. By February, 1941, their number had risen to a total of 227, but that spring a special membership committee conducted a letter-writing campaign backed up by personal calls from a lawyer designated for the purpose in each judicial district.

The results were impressive. By the annual meeting in June, 120 of them had been persuaded to pay up and the Commissioners were getting ready to go into the courts to pressure the remainder.

The courts themselves, of course, continued to be a major area of interest for the unified State Bar. Part 1 of section 24 of the 1932 unification act had, in fact, specifically assigned to the Bar the "duty" of recommending to the Legislature "such legislation relating to the courts, to matters of pleading, practice and procedure, and any other legislation which in its judgment will improve the courts and the law, or render the members of the Bar more efficient as ministers of justice and the courts more efficient as instrumentalities for its attainment." Some members believed that the quality of justice in the state courts would be best improved by the establishment of the judicial council suggested by Venable's special committee in 1930 and provided for in a draft statute by Supreme Court Justice Griffith's committee in 1931. At the 1933 annual meeting, therefore, the Board of Commissioners was asked by the members to review the proposal and report on it in 1934.

The American Judicature Society, on whose board of directors Mississippi was represented by A. T. Stovall, conducted a major campaign during the 1930s for the creation of a judicial council in every state. The June, 1934, edition of the Society's *Journal* reported approvingly that with the recent additions of New York and West Virginia half of the states now had such a council.[8] But on September 7, 1934, at the annual meeting in Hattiesburg, Commissioners Jiggitts and Dave Crawley reported that the Board after careful study, and noting that they were already authorized by the Bar Unification Act to appoint a committee "to investigate and report on the pleading practice and procedure now prevailing in the courts," had concluded that the creation of such a committee would be quicker and more effective than trying to sell the Legislature on a judicial council. In spite of an impassioned speech by Venable, who branded the committee plan "futile," the Board's recommendation was approved by 56 votes to 12.

At Natchez in 1935, the members quickly approved a commit-

8. XVIII (1934), no. 1, pp. 16–18.

tee report which recommended against creating an additional Supreme Court judgeship in the state. Far more controversial was the proposal put forward by a committee chaired by Frank Everett that the State Bar should work for passage of a constitutional amendment whereby Supreme Court justices, instead of being elected, would be selected by the governor from a list of nominees approved by the Bar as a whole, and chancellors and circuit court judges would be selected from a list of nominees approved by the lawyers in the districts they would serve. In either case the nominations would go to the governor through the Bar's commissioners and president. After some discussion the vote on the proposal was a tie: 53 to 53. It was decided, therefore, to postpone a final decision on it until the following year. In the interval there was a heated debate over its merits and demerits in the pages of the *Law Journal.* Brought up again at Greenville in 1936, it was defeated by a voice vote.

Meanwhile the state's eleven chancellors had gotten together informally at the 1935 meeting and agreed to hold a formal conference in Jackson on the first Monday in January, 1936. At the 1936 annual meeting members were told by R. W. Cutrer, who was the senior chancellor in years of service, having served for the fourth district since 1914, that he and his colleagues had formed themselves into a "Chancellors Association" with himself as chairman and D. M. Russell of the eighth district as secretary. The newly-formed group had then unanimously approved fifteen draft bills to be sent to the Legislature instituting reforms in both court procedure and the general law, which experience had taught them were badly needed. Ten of their proposals had been enacted into law by the 1936 Legislature, and five had been turned down.[9]

They had also at their January meeting adopted a set of sixty-six rules for chancery practice and procedure, embodying not only the measures adopted by the chancellors in 1921 and the changes made in them by the Chancery Practice Act of 1924 but also some new requirements which the 1930 Code had authorized them to in-

9. *Miss. LJ*, IX (1936–37), 27–30; a list of both the measures approved and those rejected is given.

stitute. It was their intention, Cutrer said, to declare the new set of rules in effect as of January 1, 1937; they asked that the State Bar give them their approval and arrange for them to be published in the *Law Journal*. After one change demanded by Dean Kimbrough, striking out "that unknown, illegitimate, unnatural phrase 'and/or' " and replacing it by "and or or," had been made, approval was given by a voice vote.[10]

The 1936 meeting at Greenville was a landmark one in many respects. For the first time W. A. Ellis of the Carthage Bar was invited to recite to members a poem he had composed in honor of the host city:

GREENVILLE

Of all the cities we have seen,
The Delta's dearest, queenliest queen
  Is Greenville by the river,
Where morning glories, wild legumes,
With cotton, corn, and clover blooms,
Shed on the air their sweet perfumes—
  Enchanting us forever.

Of all the cities we have known
Whose people we would call our own
  Were folks of high endeavor;
None can surpass this magic town,
None worthier of a noble crown,
None pulls more cash and cotton down,
  Than Greenville by the river

While men may come and men may go,
And floods may cause an overflow
  Along this mighty river,
Yet still she stands with beck'ning hands
Across the years, at God's commands.
Queen city of the Delta lands,
  O, Greenville, live forever.

Employing a wide variety of lively meters derived from the neo-classical, romantic, and modern eras, his poems were to add a note

10. *Ibid.*, pp. 31–44; a list of the rules is given.

of light, artistic entertainment to the annual meetings for the next fourteen years.

That 1936 meeting "in Greenville by the river" was also the occasion of the founding of the Junior Bar Section. The A.B.A. had established a "Junior Bar Conference" in 1934, and Dean Kimbrough, perhaps anxious to provide more of a forum within the State Bar for the bright young men who had received their training under him, was the originator of the idea in Mississippi. He picked for the task of organizing the group a 1931 graduate, Hugh N. Clayton of New Albany. Clayton got together with two Jackson friends, L. O. Smith, Jr. and W. Calvin Wells, Jr., and the three of them sat down and roughed out a set of nine by-laws for what would be "a standing committee of the Mississippi State Bar . . . known as the JUNIOR BAR SECTION of the Mississippi State Bar." Next an old typewriter was borrowed from the management of the Greenville Hotel, and Clayton, taking a seat in the lobby, typed up the by-laws using just two fingers. Then he, Smith, and Wells, assisted by John C. Satterfield, began the campaign to sell the idea to their colleagues both young and old.

Some of the older members were rather alarmed by such a novel idea. Before they would consent to it, they had to be several times reassured that the proposed group would be an integral part of the State Bar, not a separate organization that could become a competitor, and that a resolution approved by the section would by no means be regarded as binding on all of its members when they voted in the general business sessions. Such fears having been assuaged, the proposal was approved by a voice vote.[11]

Intended

> to furnish a forum for the younger lawyers, encourage and foster discussion, the interchange of ideas, and constructive action for the preservation and advancement of the ethics, prestige, and integrity of the Bar among the younger lawyers and to establish a special means whereby the younger lawyers may be induced to interest

11. Some of this information is based on an interview with H. N. Clayton, August 17, 1977.

themselves to a greater extent in the activities of the Mississippi State Bar and more materially assist in the accomplishment of its purposes and functions. . . ,

the new section, like its A.B.A. prototype, was to be for lawyers under thirty-six years of age. Hugh Clayton was immediately elected the first chairman and Jesse H. Graham of Meridian the first vice-chairman. A little later a new tradition was initiated when Chairman Clayton was elected second vice-president of the State Bar for 1936–37.

The creation of the Junior Bar Section may well have been the single most important event in the early history of the unified bar. Older lawyers, for the most part, were inclined to be content with the *status quo* and not very willing to make changes or consider new ideas, and most younger ones were understandably reluctant to speak up in the presence of their elders, let alone argue with them. Now the younger members would have an official voice in the discussion of Bar business, and the opinions of a majority of them would be formally presented.

A general spirt of optimism and confidence noticeably permeates the entire proceedings of the 1936 meeting, which began with Judge Percy Bell of Greenville remarking: "For some time our meetings were regarded without any seriousness by the public who in speaking of them seemed to stress the word 'bar.' But since we have begun to clean house, to institute some very needed reforms, to speed up our process and modernize our methods the general public has the tendency to believe that there may be something more to these meetings than mere conviviality." Much of the optimism, however, proved to be ill-founded. Just two years later, at Vicksburg in 1938, Tom Brady, Jr., of Brookhaven, after having served a year as one of the commissioners, remarked sourly that "the Bar Association has largely resolved itself into a political machine and a drinking and social organization."

For many members the greatest disappointment was the failure of their effort to reform the rules of court procedure. Venable's prediction in 1934 concerning the futility of referring the whole matter to a study committee rather than working for the creation of a judicial council proved to be well-founded. When the committee, chaired by Chief Justice Smith, prepared to make its report on the last afternoon of the 1938 meeting, those present voted instead to defer consideration of the recommended changes until the following year because so many members had already left for home. Presented again at the first session of the 1939 meeting, each of the separate recommendations was voted down by a small majority. Then, without even hearing the details of what he proposed, a motion by Venable calling for the adoption by Mississippi of the new federal rules of procedure promulgated by the United States Supreme Court in 1934 was defeated by a voice vote.

Speaking later, more in sorrow than in anger, Venable commented, "Eight long years have gone by, and if there is anything constructive that has come out of this body I do not know what it is. Every proposal is met with immediate opposition. . . ."

On the positive side, however, the members, at the same meeting, did support a resolution put forward by the Junior Bar calling on the 1940 Legislature to commission a new state Code to be ready in 1942.[12]

Meanwhile, less than three months after the final adjournment of that 1939 meeting, World War II began in Europe. The early military triumphs of the Axis powers soon gave Americans cause for grave concern, and within less than two and a half years the United States also was to be directly involved in the fighting. The bar directory for 1942 indicates that by the autumn of that year 245 Mississippi lawyers were serving in America's armed forces.

The annual meeting held at the Buena Vista in Biloxi on June 11 and 12, 1942, featured a "Victory Program." At the annual banquet on the first night, music and entertainment were provided by soldiers at the Keesler airbase. Numerous patriotic speeches were delivered during the two days. United States Senator Claude Pepper from Florida gave the annual address entitled, "A Democracy

12. Another Junior Bar suggestion, for a state bureau of identification, investigation, and statistics, was also endorsed but came to nothing.

Totally Mobilized to Win the War." Mrs. Camille Kelly, the juvenile court judge in Memphis, Tennessee, urged members to try to understand the problems of "Our Children in a World at War." Carl Marshall from nearby Gulfport, with all of the scandal and the controversy over his disbarment now almost a decade behind him, by invitation delivered an address on "The Origin, Growth and Preservation of Democracy." He was followed by Dean Kimbrough who spoke on "The Lawyer's Part in the Great Defense Problems of Today." "The Great Bar of Mississippi," he proclaimed, "with its glorious past cannot afford to delay while barbaric powers are seeking to seize and strangle the life out of our nation and reduce us to the status of a subjugated province."

After the dean has finished speaking, a motion was passed to set up a committee to prepare some suggestions as to how the war emergency could best be tackled. The next day the committee chairman, Supreme Court Justice George Ethridge, reported their five recommendations: (1) that military training be made a compulsory part of the school curriculum from the first grade through college; (2) that citizenship schools be established for immigrants; (3) that the federal government print and distribute around the world literature explaining America and the American way of life; (4) that after the war the educational process be used "to the utmost of our ability to prevent future aggression by organized governments against governments of liberty and democracy"; and (5) that the basics of law and good citizenship be taught in all schools, prisons, and other public institutions.

Some of the suggestions were really more emotional than practical, of course, but they show how strong were the feelings aroused by the war among the membership of the Bar. At the 1943 meeting in Meridian, Charles F. Engle in his presidential address denounced "the John Lewises, and the thousands upon thousands in war industries, who for personal selfish purposes, entirely disregard the welfare of those in our Armed Forces, who are giving . . . everything, even life itself, in order that our liberties may be preserved." He compared war-industry strikers to the pro–British Tories of the Revolutionary War period and suggested that "we have a right to do anything with those modern-day Tories, in order to preserve our Government, that our Fathers had a right to do against the Tories in order that this government might be founded."

A resolution was passed the following day denouncing all "racketeers and profiteers," whether employers or employees, who tried to profit from the emergency needs of the nation at war. Another resolution passed at the same time was much more practically motivated. It called on the O.P.A. to allow lawyers, as officers of the courts administering the laws of the land, sufficient gasoline to do their work.

The finances of the State Bar were a serious concern in 1943 because a measure passed by the 1942 Legislature had exempted lawyers serving with the armed forces from paying bar dues.[13] The budget had to be trimmed by about $1,500. A considerable proportion of the necessary cutback was achieved by lowering the *Law Journal's* appropriation from $2,250 for 1941–42 to $1,600 for 1942–43, with the result that only three issues were published. For 1943–44 an even smaller sum ($1,300) was budgeted, but the committee and the staff managed to put out four numbers that year anyway.

Another major saving was made with regard to the salary of the secretary-treasurer. Until the autumn of 1942 the position continued to be held by Mrs. Nevels. Earlier that same year she graduated from the Jackson School of Law and passed the Bar Exam; so once again, briefly, the secretaryship was held by a lawyer.[14] But in September she resigned to take a commission in the W.A.A.C. Meeting in the house chamber of the Capitol on September 14, the Commissioners appointed Mrs. Josephine Wright of Jackson to take Mrs. Nevel's place. With so many members of the Bar away serving in the armed forces, however, there was not so much for the secretary to do. Fortunately, in June, 1943, the Commissioners were able to persuade Miss Lottie Kuykendall, who already worked in the attorney general's office in the Capitol just

---

13. *Miss. Laws* (1942), c. 186.
14. *Mississippi Lawyer*, June, 1959, p. 13.

across the hall from the State Bar office, to take the job on a part-time basis for just $50 a month. That meant a $1,200 saving which, combined with the cut in the *Law Journal's* allotment, enabled the officers to manage the affairs of the Bar in 1943–44 on a budget of just $5,450 and in 1944–45 on $5,150, compared with $6,800 in 1940–41.

At the 1944 meeting in Jackson Ross R. Barnett, the only Bar president to date ever to be elected governor (1960–64), reported that Miss Kuykendall was performing her duties "with characteristic efficiency and ability" and that the commissioners had been holding their regular quarterly meetings as usual. The "distasteful and thankless job" of filing disbarment proceedings against three attorneys guilty of serious breaches of the ethical standards of the profession had been performed, and the previous September the Board had passed and published a resolution denouncing one provision of a recently enacted federal statute which said that the Veterans Administration, in cases where a veteran was judged incapable of handling his own affairs, was to pay any benefits due to him to his wife instead or, if he were dead, to his widow. The protection of the rights of America's fighting men, they had urged, should be left to the lawmakers of their home states.[15] All, in fact, was proceeding normally except that the Junior Bar Section, with so many of its youthful members away in the armed forces, had almost ceased to operate entirely and made no report in 1943, 1944, or 1945.

Various committees had specific war-related tasks. A Defense Committee, co-operating with the A.B.A. committee of the same name, made its services available to assist the government with legal problems. The Committee on Americanism was concerned with encouraging patriotism and keeping morale high in the state. In 1943–44 an essay contest was sponsored for high school students on the topic, "What Can the High School Students Do to Help Win the War?" The three winners were all girls. Pat Bailey of Tylertown won the first prize of a $100 war bond. Nell Roberts of Jack-

15. *Miss. LJ*, XV (1943), 319–20.

son Central got a $50 bond for being second, and Elouise Moore of Lexington, who was third, got a $25 bond. At the 1944 meeting in Jackson, future United States Senator John Stennis gave a speech on behalf of the Committee entitled "Americanism." By the autumn of 1944 a total of 356 members of the Bar were in the armed forces, according to the published Bar Directory.

Meanwhile, also at the 1944 meeting, "Certificates of Award" signed by Secretary of the Navy Forrestal and War Secretary Stimson were presented to the State Bar by senior officers from the two services in recognition of the good work being done by the 218 attorneys in the state who were participating in the Legal Assistance Program which provided low cost legal help to servicemen and their families. The attorneys' efforts were being co-ordinated at that time by a "War Work Committee" chaired by Forrest G. Cooper of Indianola.

A year later, at the 1945 meeting in Biloxi, the committee's new chairman, L. W. Maples of Gulfport, reported that, as of that June, 490 cases had been referred by legal assistance officers in the J.A.G. divisions of the services to Mississippi attorneys. About half of them had had to do with servicemen's marital problems, and seventy-five had been cases requiring a specialized knowledge of the state's property laws and rules of court procedure. With the winding down of the war in Europe, cases involving discharge regulations and demobilization procedures were beginning to be referred. Altogether the committee had mailed out 2,000 letters and spent $720 of the State Bar's funds. Soldiers, sailors, and their families had been billed strictly in accordance with their apparent ability to pay, and, if necessary, help had been provided for little or no charge.

In 1946, at the Heidelberg Hotel in Jackson, Chairman James Finch of Hattiesburg informed members that, even though the war by then had been over for ten months, the committee still had plenty of work to do helping returning servicemen with their problems. At the same time the State Bar was welcoming its own members home from the services and remembering those who would never return. Altogether eight members of the Mississippi

Bar had died for their country, including Louis M. Jiggitts, the former secretary-treasurer.[16] Also sadly missed at the 1946 meeting was Dean T. C. Kimbrough, who had died with the old year on New Year's Eve, 1945, and who was probably the only man who had had an even greater influence than Jiggitts on the development of the State Bar in Mississippi in the interwar period.

One of Kimbrough's most notable creations, the Junior Bar Section, received a new lease on life as dozens of the state's younger lawyers returned to civilian life and resumed the practice of their profession. At the 1945 meeting John Wade, a thirty-five-year-old marine corps veteran who had recently joined the University law school faculty, had been elected president of the nearly-moribund Section and had promised to get it going again. He was as good as his word, and there was a large turn-out at the group's 1946 session prior to the annual meeting of the State Bar. Founder member, Hugh N. Clayton, was there and told those present how he and others had organized the group a decade earlier at Dean Kimbrough's behest.

Another Kimbrough creation, the *Law Journal*, was helped by having its allocation raised back up to $2,000 by the Finance Committee after the several lean years during the war. The Commissioners were authorized by the members to hire a fulltime secretary-treasurer once more to handle the complex affairs of a Bar organization that now had over 1500 members. Mrs. Margaret McLean took over the position from Lottie Kuykendall for 1946–47. Mrs. Lura Ethridge held it from 1947 to 1948 and Mrs. Laura T. Reid from 1948 to the spring of 1951 when Mrs. Nevels, after a nine-year absence, was prevailed upon by the Commissioners to take the job on once again.[17] By that time the secretary's salary

---

16. Jiggitts had died of a heart attack during the war; R. J. Farley interview (August 24, 1977). The other seven memorialized at the 1946 meeting were F. L. Hawkins (Vaiden), G. R. Neblett (Shelby), P. Newman (Jackson), W. Payne (Greenville), R. Pullen (Aberdeen), G. B. Robertson (Jackson), A. J. van Blombergh (Jackson), and E. W. Wiltshire (Magnolia).

17. Commissioners' Minutes, April 5, 1951. *Mississippi Lawyer* (June 1915), p. 13. Since leaving the W.A.A.C. in 1945, Mrs. Nevels had been working in the State Tax Collector's Office.

had risen to $2,400 per year, and the *Law Journal's* allotment was up to $3,250.

Meanwhile, except for the 1948 meeting at the University in Oxford, all of the meetings for the next eight years after 1946 were held at the Buena Vista Hotel in Biloxi. They continued to be held over a two-day period in June, but, since the Junior Bar Section always held its formal annual meeting on the afternoon of the day before the opening of the State Bar meeting, for many of the members they were in fact still three-day affairs as they had been before the war.

W. A. Ellis of Carthage had continued down through the war years to recite one or more poems specially written for the occasion at each annual meeting. At the 1948 one, in a resolution moved by W. N. Ethridge of Oxford, he was formally commended "for his services as Poet Laureate." His 1949 poem on "American Freedom" was to be his last, however. His name appears on the list of recently-deceased members of the Bar commemorated in the proceedings of the 1950 meeting. No new laureate was appointed to take his place perhaps partly because, in the sophisticated, post-war world, where the best professional talents could be heard daily by everyone on the radio or even seen on television, amateur poetry recitals had rather gone out of fashion. Amateur music recitals ceased to be a feature of the annual meetings after 1942, and motorcar outings were no longer a part of the entertainment provided by local hosts. Another sign of the changing times in 1948–49 was the decision by President Phil Stone to add to the eleven committees then in existence a new one on aviation, whose members were to consider the legal implications of the age of air travel.[18]

New ages bring with them new problems. One of the major

18. Phil Stone is remembered today primarily as the friend and patron of amateur aviator and Nobel Prize winning novelist, William Faulkner. The eleven committees already in existence were those on Administrative Law, Budget and Finance, the Judicial Conference, the *Law Journal*, Legal Education and Admissions to the Bar, Procedural Reform, Memorials, Arrangements for the Annual Meeting, Program for the Annual Meeting, Resolutions, and the Study Committee.

ones after World War II was how to preserve the peace that had been so dearly won. Members of the Mississippi Bar in 1947 were optimistic that the United Nations would be able to enforce the rule of law around the globe. At the 1947 meeting they passed a resolution, drafted by Judge John C. Stennis who a few months later would be elected to the seat in the U.S. Senate left vacant by the death of Bilbo, endorsing American participation in the world organization.

At home in Mississippi there were problems too in the postwar age. The state did not suffer a severe economic recession as it had after World War I, partly no doubt because agriculture was coming to be more evenly balanced with light industry and nearly everything economic no longer depended solely on the price of cotton. But modern industry is usually accompanied by trade union activity, and Mississippi like most of the South did not look upon trade unions in a very favorable light. At the 1950 annual meeting a resolution was passed condemning President Truman's solicitor general, Philip B. Perlman, for having said that the federal Fifth Circuit Court seemed inclined to deny the National Labor Relations Board due process of law. For making such an attack on a court, the resolution urged, Perlman should "be dealt with and disciplined very sternly. . . ."

Another problem for the state, and another cause for dissatisfaction with the federal government, was the whole question of race relations. Even though the 1940 census showed (for the first time since 1840) a white majority in Mississippi, the issue of whites versus blacks after the war became more heated than it had been for several decades. There was no trouble within the ranks of the Bar itself, probably because the 1941 Bar list (the last one to provide such information) included only five "colored" lawyers, all of them practicing in Jackson; however, among the people and in the political arena there was heated controversy. One reason for it, as Hugh N. Clayton remarked to the revived Junior Bar in 1946, was that the events of the war years had caused blacks to entertain higher hopes and expectations. Many blacks in the armed forces had seen the world, and some of them had marched into Germany, others had landed in Japan, as conquering heroes. Many had gone off to lucrative jobs in unsegregated northern industrial cities. The ruling Democratic party, beginning under Roosevelt, had organized and had come to rely on, the black urban vote. To attract and keep that vote, policies were being pursued in Washington that most white Mississippians, including a majority of the members of the Bar, in spite of their traditional identification with the Democratic party, found highly distasteful.

As early as 1943, while the war was still being fought, concern had been voiced at the annual meeting over a bill then being debated in Congress which would have eliminated all poll tax requirements in federal elections. It was suggested that southern governors ought to begin working together to nominate a Democratic candidate for president in 1944 who would allow "fair and decent treatment for Southern Ideals and Southern interests." Roosevelt, it was remarked, "showed no pride of race" and seemingly "intended to do his best to destroy segregation." After the war President Truman appeared to be even more determined to destroy the South's way of life. His setting up of the Civil Rights Commission in 1946 and his desegregation of the armed forces by executive order were deeply resented. Fearful that the Missourian might remain in office as long as Roosevelt had, the members at the 1947 meeting resolved unanimously that Mississippi should "promptly ratify" the proposed Twenty-second Amendment to the U.S. Constitution limiting a president to a maximum of two terms.

They hoped, in fact, that Truman would not even be elected to a second term, and by the time of the 1948 meeting most members of the Bar, like most white Mississippians, were dedicated Dixiecrats. One speaker, taking note of the fair employment practices act, the new anti-poll tax act, and the new anti-lynching law proposed by the Civil Rights Commission, saw a return of Reconstruction coming. "Is the South," he asked his hearers, "to be called upon to ENDURE A SECOND TRAGIC ERA?"

Later the members present unanimously passed a resolution

in which they firmly stated that they were dedicated to the preservation of states rights, that they objected to

> the so-called civil rights bills now pending in Congress and pledge ourselves to the task of restoring to our party the philosophy of the first platform of the Democratic Party adopted in 1840 as follows: "Congress has no power under the Constitution to interfere with or control the domestic institutions of the several states and that such states are the sole and proper judges of everything appertaining to their own affairs not prohibited by the Constitution." Such pronouncement is the cornerstone of the original Democratic Party and we believe that that platform and that philosophy should be maintained as the Democratic Party platform of today.

But, in spite of all that the Dixiecrats and Thomas E. Dewey could do, Truman was elected to a second term.

Meanwhile, there were other federal policies besides those dealing with race relations that were unpopular with Mississippi's lawyers. At the 1947 meeting, noting that the Supreme Court in Washington had ruled in the *United States* v. *California* that all tidewater lands belonged to the U.S.A., the members had passed a resolution calling on Congress to pass whatever legislation was needed to convey them back to the various states. Commenting on this decision in his 1949 presidential address, Phil Stone remarked: "My principal objection is that [it] seems to be one more of a great and growing group, one more of the many decisions, one more of the many executive and administrative orders, one more of the several acts of Congress, that have for many years driven political and economic power more and more tightly into centralization in the Federal Government." Unwanted legislation in Congress could be, and usually was, filibustered to death by the South's representatives in the Senate. But if the United States Supreme Court, which the Bar had hailed back in the 1920s as the reliable champion of states' rights, was now taking a different attitude, there might be serious problems ahead.

Meanwhile the condition of Mississippi's courts and lawyers

continued, as always, to be the major concern of members of the State Bar. Besides the problem of race relations, Clayton suggested to the Junior Bar in 1946 two other issues to which they should give very serious consideration: first, the qualifications required for admission to the Bar and second, the need for reform in court procedures.

Although suggested procedural reform measures had been defeated at Biloxi in 1939, it had been by only a very narrow margin, and many members remained hopeful that at some time in the future they would yet be put into effect. Meanwhile other kinds of law reform were also pushed. W. C. Wells had been able to report in 1940 that certain constitutional and statutory changes in the state's mortmain laws, recommended by the Bar, which made it much easier for Mississippians to include bequests to charities and schools in their wills, had been approved by the Legislature.[19] And in 1941 the Bar had endorsed a series of changes in the federal criminal code that had been recommended by the A.B.A., except for one that called for including pistols and revolvers under the provisions of the National Firearms Act.

With regard to procedural reforms the study committee in 1942 had recommended deferring any further consideration of them for the duration of the war, but the 1943 study committee had felt differently. They had urged that a plan for at least the partial adoption of the new federal rules by the state's courts be published in the *Law Journal* and given serious consideration by every member of the Bar. And in fact the proposed changes had been discussed during 1943–44 at chancellors' and circuit court judges' meetings and at local bar association gatherings. The Mississippi Federation of Business and Professional Women's Clubs had declared their support for them. In the 1944 Legislature, however, six bills embodying the proposed changes, although approved by the Senate, had died in the House of Representatives.[20]

The 1944–45 Study Committee was undiscouraged and urged that the Bar continue to press for the rejected measures. In 1947

19. *Miss. Laws* (1940), c. 318.
20. *Miss. LJ*, XVI (1944), 302–03.

the Junior Bar Section presented to the annual meeting a new single bill incorporating them, which its membership had unanimously endorsed. When some members of the Bar objected to it because it would confer on the state Supreme Court the power to change procedural rules, William Keady of Greenville, who had served as chairman of the Judiciary Committee in the previous Senate, remarked that, if the changing of the rules were left up to the legislators, it would take at least a generation before it would be done. So the proposed bill was approved.

The 1948 Legislature did not pass it, though they did at last pass the Workman's Compensation Bill called for by the Bar Association in 1919 and also enacted several statutes embodying important procedural changes that would shorten trials and reduce the expenses for parties engaged in suits in the state courts. The "old rigid common law forms of pleas and special defenses" were abolished, and instead all matters of defense were to be "incorporated without formality into one answer designed to narrow and identify the actual contested issues without spending valuable court time proving facts that should be readily admitted by the opposite party." Also defendants were in the future to be required to answer within thirty days of a process being served or on the first day of the return term, whichever would be earlier.[21] Such a partial success was gratifying, but far from completely satisfactory. In 1948–49 a Procedural Reform committee of the Bar began work on a new bill containing those provisions that the Legislature had rejected. And at each of the next three annual meetings, in 1949, 1950, and 1951, their draft was approved by majorities of those who attended. The campaign was continuing.

Meanwhile, another piece of proposed reform legislation, originated by the Junior Bar and approved at the 1947 meeting, had met with even less success. Dealing with admissions to the bar, it first of all proposed a major change in the make-up of the Board

21. *Miss. Laws* (1948), cc. 229–30. McLemore, II, 384. It is interesting to note that in 1850 the Legislature had abolished all of the Common Law forms of pleading, but they were reinstated in the 1857 Code. See V. A. Griffith, "The New Mississippi Civil Practice Act: Its Background and Effect," *Miss. LJ*, XX (1947–48), 3–6; see also Robert and Jan Patterson, "A Plan for Procedural Reform in Mississippi," *ibid.*, XLII (1970–71), 294.

of Bar Admissions. Since 1916 the board had consisted of three attorneys, one from each of the Supreme Court districts, appointed by the governor for two-year terms. The proposal was that it be composed of the chief justice of the Supreme Court or one of the other justices designated by him, the dean of the University law school or some other faculty member designated by him, and three practicing attorneys chosen by the Supreme Court out of each of the three districts for three-year terms. Having it so constituted would go a long way towards restoring to the judicial branch that control over entrance to the profession that it had enjoyed in the nineteenth century.[22] The secretary-treasurer of the State Bar was to serve as secretary to the Board, and two years of general college plus three years of training at a law school, which generally met A.A.L.S. standards and was not "operated primarily as a commercial enterprise," were to be a prerequisite for admission. All of those present were in favor of the first two parts of the draft bill, but discussion on the third part concerning educational requirements became quite heated. It even became acrimonious when it was suggested that certain Jackson lawyers were only opposing it because they had a financial interest in the Jackson School of Law. The charge was indignantly denied by the accused, who insisted that their only concern was for the "poor boy who is struggling for an opportunity to practice our noble profession." Finally, those present approved the draft measure by eighty-three votes to forty-nine, but it got nowhere with the Legislature. Bar admission requirements and procedures remained as they had been.

Understandably, admission to the bar was more of an issue in the Junior Bar Section, many of whose members were still struggling to build up a practice, than it was among the older, established members of the Bar. For the same reason the Section's members were usually the ones most concerned about the issue of the unauthorized practice of law. At the Section's first full meeting in 1937 they had unanimously passed a motion asking the state's judges to warn court clerks, notaries public, and similar officials

---

22. *Miss. Laws* (1916), c. 107. Prior to 1916, admissions to the bar were controlled by the Supreme Court and/or circuit judges and chancellors; Codes, 1824–1906, *passim*.

against the temptation to try to function as amateur attorneys. In 1938 they had persuaded the annual meeting of the State Bar to approve a draft bill prohibiting the practice of law either by non-lawyers or by judges.

That bill was never passed by the Legislature, perhaps because it did not really need to be. The 1942 Code clearly stated that it was a misdemeanor for people in either category to engage in legal practice.[23] The problem, nevertheless, remained a real one apparently. At the 1950 meeting, again at the request of the Junior Bar, a resolution was passed calling on the secretary to mail out to newspapers, court clerks, justices of the peace, real estate agents, insurance adjusters, and title guaranty association members "a statement as to what is considered the unauthorized practice of law" and pointing out what is prohibited by statute as set forth in the Code. The Bar, however, refused a request from the Section for an extra allotment of $500 to be spent in the campaign against unauthorized practice because the budget and finance committee had not approved it in advance and money was tight.

As a matter of fact, the largest single group engaged in the unauthorized practice of law in the state in the years immediately after World War II probably were those lawyers who, in defiance of section 25 of the 1932 Unified Bar Act, continued to pursue their profession without paying their bar dues. Threats of disbarment combined with cajoling appeals had considerably reduced the number of delinquents in 1941, it is true, but a few years later the number had crept up again. The state Bar list for 1951 indicates that, out of Mississippi's 2,035 lawyers, 149 had not paid. In 1949–50, under President R. W. Thompson, Jr. of Gulfport, disbarment proceedings had been begun in the chancery courts against all the delinquents. One case had been promptly tried, and the chancellor after a full hearing had declared the 1932 law constitutional and ordered the lawyer concerned suspended from practicing until he paid. Unfortunately, "because of a tragic circumstance," that case was never appealed to the Supreme Court.[24]

---

23. Secs. 8668, 8682.
24. *Miss. LJ*, XXIII (1952–53), 312.

At the 1952 annual meeting, however, President Quitman Ross of Laurel had good news for the members. In August, 1951, the chancery court of Jones County, in a similar case, had declared the 1932 law unconstitutional. The seventeen commissioners by a unanimous vote had resolved to appeal that ruling to the state Supreme Court. And just eleven days earlier, on June 9, 1952, the court had announced its decision. With regard to the *Board of Bar Commissioners of the Mississippi State Bar* v. *Collins*, the justices had ruled that the State Bar was "not a private corporation" and that the Unified Bar Act was "not a local or private act to benefit a corporation, nor to regulate practice in the courts," but rather had "a general application to all active lawyers in the state." They had also ruled that the act did "not represent an encroachment by the legislature upon the powers of the judiciary."[25] These rulings meant that lawyers must pay their bar dues in the future or face swift disbarment.

Ross had more good news. In 1951 the members had approved a recommendation, coming both from the Commissioner's Study Committee and the Junior Bar Section, that the Legislature be requested to raise bar dues from $5, which had been the rate ever since the state's first bar association had been founded in Natchez in 1821, to $10 per year. The object was to provide sufficient funds for "not only carrying on the routine business of the Association but also active committee work in the interests of our profession within itself and in its relationship to the public." None of the other measures urged by the Bar had been passed by the 1952 session; however, they had passed that one, and the governor had signed it on April 15.[26] So, with its constitutionality affirmed, and its income assured and now almost doubled, the unified State Bar of Mississippi in its twentieth year could look to the future with a fair degree of confidence.

25. *Miss. Reports*, 214:782. *Southern Reporter* (25), 59:351. A.J.S. *Cit. and Bibl.*, p. 16.
26. *Miss. Laws* (1952), c. 241.

VI

The Recent Past—The Organization

1952–1976

In 1952, the year that the state Supreme Court upheld its constitutionality, the unified Mississippi State Bar was twenty years old and approaching the traditional age of legal maturity. A new generation of leaders was taking over as the second half of the century commenced, and possible alterations and improvements in the organization's structure were being considered. Not only younger members, however, but also some of those who had occupied positions of leadership in the recent past were suggesting changes that their own experiences had persuaded them were badly needed.

Former president Phil Stone (1948–49) for example, writing in the May, 1950, issue of the *Law Journal*, had a number of important recommendations to make.[1] With regard to the Board of Bar Commissioners he noted that some of the seventeen districts preferred to re-elect the same man year after year while others would always choose a different man from a different county. Neither practice, in his opinion, was ideal. Some continuity was certainly needed on the Board, and there was also certainly a need for new members from different backgrounds and with original ideas. He proposed, therefore, that the Commissioners serve for staggered terms of three or four years duration and then be replaced with someone from a different county in their district. Thus a body of lawyers would be built up around the state "who knew how the association was run," with the result that "in a few years,

1. *Miss. LJ*, II (1949–50), 372–78.

any lawyer in any county who wanted to know something about the association would have in his county a man who had served on the commission and who could inform him."

Stone also called for two complaint commissioners instead of just one: "This is too great a burden for one man," he wrote. He also felt that the Junior Bar Section needed more than just one half-day session before the main annual meeting to carry out their "splendid work," and he thought that the annual meetings themselves ought to be held on a Thursday and Friday rather than, as was the custom, on a Friday and Saturday, because country lawyers needed to be in their offices on Saturday mornings. Presidents of the State Bar, he urged, should always be elected in the first full business day when most members were likely to be present. Previous service as a Commissioner should be a prerequisite for the presidency, so that every president would be familiar with how the Association operated; and once a president was elected, he should have all of his committees appointed by August so that they could put in a full year's work. Also members ought to be rotated on and off the various committees to keep them from getting stale. Every committee should include some old members, some young members, and, if possible, some members from the Legislature so as to have "on the floor of each house . . . informed and effective spokesmen for the various programs of the association."

Stone's final piece of advice was that an endowment fund be created to receive gifts and bequests, "the income from which could be used to promote the interests of the lawyers of Mississippi."

Three years later some further pieces of advice were offered by Charles B. Snow of Jackson in his presidential address. He told members present at the 1952 annual meeting that the State Bar offices in the New Capitol building were "wholly inadequate," consisting as they did of "a little, one-room cubby hole, at the south entrance on the second floor." The office equipment was old and obsolete, and most of it was borrowed. He hoped that more adequate quarters and more modern equipment might soon be obtained. He also hoped that in the future State Bar presidents could enjoy a closer relationship with local bar associations around the state than he had during his year in office. His main recommendation, however, was that the first vice-president be replaced by a president-elect. The president-elect would attend commissioners' meetings and generally serve as assistant to the incumbent president, so that when he succeeded to the presidency a year later there could be much greater "continuity in ideas and plans and performance."

During the course of the two and a half decades that followed, almost all of the suggestions made by Stone and Snow were to be carried out, with the result that by the mid-1970's the organization and operations of the State Bar had been greatly improved, transformed, and expanded.

On June 22, 1956, at the Hotel Edwards in Jackson, Joe H. Daniel of Jackson reported to the annual meeting about the proposals agreed on by a Committee on the Revision of the State Bar Act and By-laws, appointed by President John C. Satterfield (1955–56). Briefly, Chairman Daniel said, they wanted to recommend (1) that the Legislature be asked to authorize the State Bar to set its own dues; (2) that the by-laws be revised so as to have the first vice-president automatically succeed to the office of president; (3) that the method of selecting the sites of annual meetings be changed; (4) that the duties of the complaints commissioner be transferred to a Complaints Committee; (5) that the by-law prohibiting commissioners from serving on committees be repealed; (6) that the Legislature be asked to amend the Act so as to provide for staggered terms for commissioners; and (7) that a minimum number of standing committees be provided for in the by-laws, with a general outlining of their various functions and some continuity in their membership.

Those present evidently agreed with the statement contained in the first proposal "that the Bar Association is competent to govern itself in the fixing of its dues," for they voted their approval of the idea. The Legislature, however, has never, to date, been willing to go along with it. The members also approved the fourth and fifth proposals, establishing a Complaints Committee and allowing commissioners to serve on committees, and the seventh, calling for a more fixed and organized committee structure. But a motion approving the sixth proposal, calling for commissioners to serve staggered terms, was tabled. And the second and third proposals, whereby individual members and local bar groups would be polled by mail before each future annual meeting on their choice for president and vice-president and the meeting-place for the following year, were voted down. Finally a motion by Daniel was approved which salvaged one element of the second proposal by amending article I of the by-laws so as to provide for the automatic succession of the first vice-president to the presidency.

The new arrangement was put into effect the following year. W. S. Henley of Hazlehurst, who had been elected first vice-president for 1956–57, was unanimously elected to succeed M. M. Roberts of Hattiesburg as president for 1957–58. Three years later, at the 1960 meeting in the King Edward Hotel[2] in Jackson, what had become by then the pure formality of electing the next president was dispensed with. The outgoing president, Hugh N. Clayton, simply announced that president-elect David Cottrell, Jr. of Gulfport would assume the position of president upon the adjournment of the convention. In 1959 Cottrell had been elected to the position of "first vice-president"; now, in 1960, Sherwood W. Wise of Jackson was elected as "first vice-president and president elect." Meanwhile, the custom had been long-since established that the outgoing president of the Junior Bar Section was nominated by his successor and elected unopposed to the office of second vice-president. At the 1963 meeting, in the Heidelberg Hotel at Jackson, article I of the by-laws was again amended so as to bring it fully into accord with the procedures by then already being followed in the election of the president and vice-presidents.

Mrs. Alice Nevels, meanwhile, continued to serve as secretary-treasurer, assisted by Mrs. Lillian Sadler as chief stenographer. In 1958 it was apparently understood that Mrs. Nevels was going to retire, and a resolution was passed at the annual meeting that year thanking her for her long years of faithful service; however, a year

2. Formerly known as the "Hotel Edwards."

later she was still on the job, and another resolution was passed endorsing everything that had been said about her the year before. Mrs. Nevels, in fact, in spite of some health problems, evidently found it impossible to leave her exacting, but also exciting and challenging job, for she stayed on for another seven years.

In 1963 President C. Sidney Carlton of Sumner told the members:

> Mrs. Nevels is not only the Secretary-Treasurer of the Mississippi State Bar, she is . . . Secretary of the Board of Bar Admissions, Secretary of the Junior Bar Section, . . . Mother confessor of the individual lawyers of the State of Mississippi, the head of her family, a devoted mother, and a doting and admirable grandmother, and she is also a delightful and lovable person, and as far as I am concerned, she is MRS. MISSISSIPPI STATE BAR.

Obviously she was more than just a secretary or even a secretary-treasurer. That same year the by-laws were amended changing her title to "executive director and secretary-treasurer."

When Mrs. Nevels did finally retire in 1966, a motion was passed at that year's annual meeting expressing the members' "sincere thanks and appreciation for [her] outstanding, efficient, courteous and dedicated services." She was succeeded as executive director by George H. Van Zant, a native Jacksonian, who from 1959 to 1966 had held the position of business promotion manager for the Jackson Chamber of Commerce. Although he was not a lawyer at the time of his appointment to the executive directorship, Van Zant graduated from the Jackson School of Law in 1971 and was admitted to the Bar in 1972. So the custom of having a lawyer in the position was maintained.

By the time Van Zant began his duties, the State Bar office had long since moved out of the "one-room cubby hole" that President Snow had complained about thirteen years before. Less than a year after Snow had voiced his complaint, in fact, Mrs. Nevels, by vigorous lobbying, had secured permission to move into a much larger office on the first floor of the Capitol. Reporting on the move to the 1954 annual meeting, President Jerome S. Hafter of Greenville had observed that many state bar associations around the country were constructing their own headquarters buildings and he suggested that serious consideration be given to establishing a fund to build a new headquarters for the Mississippi State Bar. Three years later, however, plans were being made to build a "Supreme Court Building . . . on a suitable plot in the vicinity of the new Capitol." In addition to a Supreme Court chamber and offices, its backers also intended that it should house the State Law Library, the attorney general's department, and the State Bar headquarters. A "Supreme Court Building Committee" reported at both the 1958 and 1959 annual meetings, and in the latter year members were urged to use any influence they had with the members of the 1960 Legislature to persuade them to appropriate funds for the planned structure.[3]

It was not until the extraordinary reapportionment session held in the winter of 1966–67, however, that the Legislature finally voted the money to build what was to be called the "Carroll Gartin Justice Building."[4] At the 1969 annual meeting at the Heidelberg Hotel in Jackson, President C. Curtis of Clarksdale reported that during the preceding year he and the Commissioners had been considering where to obtain the funds needed to furnish and equip the offices to be allotted to the State Bar in the new structure. Meanwhile, in December, 1969, Van Zant and his staff moved into a set of offices in the old Robert E. Lee Hotel which had recently been acquired as a state office building. And a few weeks later the 1970 session of the Legislature amended the Unified Bar Act to allow "that the State Bar Association office may be at a place other than the Capitol Building," though with the stipulation that the secretary must continue to maintain his office "at the seat of government."[5]

President Curtis had told the 1969 meeting that he was "afraid it will be some years before we can be housed in the contemplated

3. *Miss. LJ*, XXIX (1957–58), 502–03; XXX (1958–59), 573–74.
4. *Miss. Laws* (1966–ext.), c. 21. Lt. Gov. Carroll Gartin, a member of the Laurel bar, died in office in December, 1966.
5. *Miss. Laws* (1970), c. 352.

Justice Building," and he suggested that the members "give serious thought to constructing [their own] building." By the time of the 1970 meeting in Biloxi the members apparently were convinced of the wisdom of his recommendation, for they passed a resolution requesting and authorizing the Board of Commissioners "to appoint the necessary committee and take the necessary action to obtain a grant of state land in Jackson . . . from the . . . Legislature, and to prepare plans for a suitable Bar Center Building, and to solicit and raise the necessary funds, and to proceed within its means to the construction of a permanent Mississippi Bar Center." When the Carroll Gartin building was finally opened in 1973, as things turned out, there was only enough room in it to meet the needs of the Supreme Court and other legal departments of the state. So the State Bar offices continued to be located in the Robert E. Lee Building until January, 1977, when they finally moved into their new headquarters at 620 North State Street, just a few blocks northeast of the Capitol.

Although both the 1932 and 1970 statutes provided that the Board of Bar Commissioners might meet anywhere they chose, most meetings in modern times have been held in Jackson at the State Bar office. Very often, however, more than the customary four meetings a year have been necessary; for example, seven meetings were held in 1962–63, five in 1965–66, and seven again in 1970. In 1959 under President Clayton, the practice was begun of having the two immediate former presidents attend board meetings in order to provide greater continuity. At the 1967 meeting in Biloxi, John T. Armstrong of Hazlehurst, in his presidential address, once again revived the suggestion that continuity would be better promoted by having the Commissioners serve for staggered, three-year terms. Perhaps because many members wanted frequent opportunities to be elected, and those who were elected did not wish to be committed to a long term of service, the proposal continued to be rejected. Armstrong's other suggestion, that the election of commissioners be scheduled somewhere midway through the program rather than at the last session when many members had already left to go home, was also ignored.

Two years later, at the 1969 meeting in Jackson, President Curtis made the same two suggestions. He reminded members that usually only some 250 to 300 of them, or about ten percent of the current total Bar membership of 2,600, usually took part in the election of officers. Observing that most state bars had a nominating committee system and elected their officials by ballot, he recommended that the whole process be reviewed and overhauled. Finally, in 1972, the practice was initiated of having two names put forward for the office of president-elect by a nominating committee made up of the past presidents, with additional nominations also being accepted from the floor. The election continued to be held at the closing session of the annual meeting, however, until 1977 when for the first time a secret ballot of all the members was conducted by mail in the spring. Three-year, staggered terms for the commissioners were initiated at last in 1976, and now they too are elected by a mail ballot of all the lawyers in each circuit court district.

The Commissioners in 1959 found themselves faced with the ever-recurring problem of members who were delinquent in paying their dues. The Budget and Finance Committee reported that year that 71 attorneys owed a total of $1,595, and they called on the Board to formulate "a definite plan of dealing with these delinquents." A start might be made, they suggested, by taking their names off the *Law Journal* mailing list. Steps were taken, and by 1963 President Carlton was able to inform the members meeting at Jackson that only nine of their colleagues were in arrears and that suits had been filed against them "asking for an injunction prohibiting their practice of law until such dues are paid and asking for a monetary judgment in the amount of the delinquent dues." By the early 1970s a regular and efficient procedure had been worked out, whereby the delinquent received a letter sent to him by certified mail notifying him that he had just sixty days to pay what was in arrears and, if he failed to pay before that time was up, the judges in his district would automatically notify him of his suspension. As a result by the mid-1970s fewer than one percent of a total bar membership of some 3,000 were to be found in the delinquent category.

Members who did not pay their dues were inevitably a matter of concern because the Mississippi State Bar during the third quarter of the twentieth century continued to have serious budgeting problems. The raising of the dues to $10 by the Legislature in 1952 meant that it was possible to plan a budget for 1952–53 of $16,250, almost twice that of the previous year ($8,950). The secretary's salary was by then up to $3,600 a year, however, and $1,500 was being paid for additional office help and $1,800 for office expenses. The *Law Journal* was getting $4,600 and the Junior Bar Section $1,000. The commissioners were allotted $900 for their expenses, and $750 was provided for the various committees. Most of the rest of the money was to go for travel expenses: $500 for the secretary to go to the A.B.A. annual meeting, $350 for delegates to the American Judicial Conference, and $300 for delegates to the Conference on Uniform State Laws. For 1953–54 the committees' allotment was raised to $2,000 and that year for the first time the president was to be given a stipend amounting to $250 to help cover his expenses. Also furniture and equipment were needed for the new, larger office on the first floor of the Capitol, so $400 was budgeted for that. The money for the new items was provided by cutting the *Law Journal*, which had asked for $1,000 more, back by $1,000 to $3,600. However, the *Journal* seems not to have suffered from the cut for it finished the following fiscal year with a surplus of over $300, and for 1954–55 half of the cut made the previous year was restored, so that they got $4,000.

Another $4,000 item in the budget for 1954–55 was for the work of the new Board of Bar Admissions created by the 1954 Legislature.[6] The secretary of the State Bar was to serve also as secretary to the new board. Candidates taking the bar exam were to pay a fee of $25 to the secretary, and she was to pay $20 per day out of that to the examiners for their work, retaining the balance to cover administrative expenses.

For the next few years the budgets, which now totalled around $20,000 annually, were quite adequate to meet the needs of the State Bar. In 1956 the secretary's salary was raised to $3,900, and

6. *Miss. Laws* (1954), c. 213.

the expense account allowed the commissioners was expanded to $1,500. Two years later both the secretary and the stenographer were given further raises of $300 each. In order to do so, however, $500 less was to be made available for committees than in the previous year, and the *Law Journal*, which had been given $4,750 in 1957, was to have its allotment cut back once again to $4,000. The Budget and Finance Committee warned that further cuts would be needed the following year "unless, in the meantime, some plan of voluntary contribution from the members is promulgated, or unless some relief is granted by the Legislature, including an increase in the annual dues." The Junior Bar Section recommended that each member be asked to contribute an additional $15, and finally a resolution did pass asking for voluntary contributions of $10. At the 1959 meeting a similar request was approved in order to help meet an estimated budget of $22,675.

The 1960 session of the Legislature at last came to the rescue by passing three important statutes.[7] One of them once again doubled the annual dues payable by lawyers to the State Bar to $20. Another required non-resident attorneys who wished to be licensed to practice in Mississippi courts to pay an application fee of $50 to the Bar. And a third raised the fee for taking the bar exam to $50.

Beginning that same year the State Bar's budgets ceased to be published along with the other reports in the *Law Journal*, and so it becomes more difficult to find out the details; however, inflation apparently very soon began to undermine the situation once again. By 1966 President Orma R. Smith of Corinth was telling the members that once more dues needed to be raised, and he suggested a figure of $40. Medical doctors, he pointed out, were paying $50 to their state organization and dentists were paying $44. The following year President Armstrong reported a budget deficit of several thousand dollars. If dues were not raised, he warned, some State Bar activities would have to be curtailed in 1968. Meanwhile, he greatly appreciated the additional contributions that some members were sending in along with their dues. Then, in the spring of

7. *Miss. Laws* (1960), cc. 286, 288, 289.

1968, the Legislature stepped in again and raised the dues to $30. That increase proved adequate for the time being, but President Curtis noted in 1969 that it probably would not be so for long. He reminded members that $40 was the national average for state bar dues.

Two years later, President William A. Bacon of Jackson told the members meeting at the new Broadwater Beach Hotel in Biloxi that $30 was no longer even adequate for the Bar's needs and that the dues paid by Mississippi lawyers were by then the lowest in the nation. When the Legislature did consent to raise them to $40 in 1973, even that amount was not entirely adequate. Consequently, three years later in 1976, they were again raised to a rate of $60 for those who had been practicing for more than three years and $45 for those in their first three years of practice. How long those rates will continue to be "adequate" remains to be seen.

In addition to its 3,000 or so dues-paying members, and the federal and state judges, the Mississippi State Bar included some honorary members among its ranks by the early 1960s. At the 1957 meeting a resolution was passed conferring honorary membership on Mrs. Julia Bailey Starnes, who had been serving as the state law librarian since 1940, and in 1959 the same distinction was conferred on both Kenneth Toler, Jackson correspondent of the Memphis *Commercial Appeal*, and Governor James Orval Faubus of Arkansas, who had recently earned worldwide notoriety for his strong resistance to school desegregation. In 1960 prominent New York City lawyer, Whitney North Seymour, president-elect of the A.B.A., was admitted to honorary membership together with his wife.

Mrs. Starnes was not only the first non-lawyer but also the first woman ever to be elected an honorary member of the Mississippi State Bar. Five years earlier, in 1952, Miss Lena C. Zama of Hazlehurst had broken down another major sex-barrier by being elected as the fourteenth district's representative on the Board of Commissioners. And three years after that, in 1955, Mrs. Zelma W. Price of Greenville had become the state's first woman judge when she was elected to preside over the county court of Washington

County. By 1962, though it is impossible to tell how many of them were actually practicing, the names of some fifty-four women appear in the State Bar list. A decade later the 1972 list shows that the number had almost doubled: ninety-six women belonged to the Mississippi State Bar, including twelve who lived out of the state. That was the year that Lenore L. Prather of Columbus took her seat on the bench as chancellor for the fourteenth district, and a year later, in 1973, Betty B. Tucker of Jackson became one of the chancellors for the fifth district. As the twentieth century moved towards its final quarter, in fact, women were coming into their own in the legal profession in Mississippi, not just as members but as leaders in the profession.[8]

Not all of the women working in law offices, of course, are members of the Bar, for few lawyers of either sex could operate professionally for very long without the aid of their secretaries. At the 1960 meeting Mrs. Hazel Crimes of Jackson was invited to speak to the members about the work of the National Association of Legal Secretaries, for whom she was the Mississippi state director. Founded in 1929 in Long Beach, California, the N.A.L.S. by 1950 had 160 chapters around the United States. In 1959 the Jackson Legal Secretaries Association had affiliated with it and received a charter as a chapter. The organization, Mrs. Crimes emphasized, was not a union but rather a professional association. "Just as our employer serves his profession by being a member of the Bar," she said, "so we can serve our profession as a legal secretary by being a part of N.A.L.S." She urged all those present to encourage their secretaries to join the association and to form local chapters. Three years later she reported again to the members on the progress she was making, and in 1964 Mrs. Flora Blount, president of the newly-established Mississippi Association of Legal Secretaries (M.A.L.S.), told the annual meeting at Gulfport about her group and its work.

---

8. Future Lt. Gov. Evelyn Gandy had served as the first woman editor of the *Law Journal* in 1942. No doubt before the end of the century we will see the first woman president of the State Bar and the first woman on the state Supreme Court.

That 1964 annual meeting at the Edgewater Gulf Hotel in Gulfport was the last to be held in the city on the Coast where the first annual meeting had been held in 1906. The 1966 and 1969 meetings were both held in Jackson, the birthplace of the organized State Bar, but the closing of first the King Edward Hotel in 1968 and then the Heidelberg Hotel in 1972 meant that the state's capital city by the mid-70s could no longer accommodate the 500 or so members, with their wives and other guests, who regularly attended the Bar meetings. The meetings in 1965, 1967, 1968, and 1970 were held at Biloxi. In 1970, however, the members could not convene as they had for decades when they went to Biloxi at the Buena Vista Hotel, where manager Jimmy Love always entertained them most hospitably and took care of all their needs; on the night of Monday, August 17, 1969, the Buena Vista had been irreparably damaged by the 190-mile-an-hour winds of Hurricane Camille. The hotel's pavillion situated on the pier, which had housed more Mississippi State Bar meetings than any other auditorium in the state, had been totally obliterated by a giant tidal wave and with it the lives of a group of foolhardy revellers who had ignored official advice to evacuate inland and had stayed behind to stage a "hurricane party." Instead the Broadwater Beach Hotel, which had "weathered the storm well" and suffered only minor damage in spite of nearly ten feet of water in the lobby, became the Bar's new headquarters for all of the subsequent annual meetings.[9]

A decade earlier, at the 1961 meeting at the ill-fated Buena Vista in Biloxi, Hugh Clayton had offered a motion to the effect that article V of the by-laws be amended so as to empower the commissioners to select the annual meeting site in the future as well as the dates in June when it would be held, making the selection two years in advance. After much discussion the motion passed with the proviso that it would not apply until the time came for the selection of the 1965 meeting place. So, beginning in 1963,

9. *Clarion Ledger*, August 19, 1969, p. 14, col. 3; August 20, 1969, p. 14, col. 6.

the choice was no longer to be left to the few rank and file members still present and voting at the final business session on the last day.[10]

The new arrangement meant that more long-range planning of annual meeting programs was possible. From 1952 to 1958 several hundred dollars had been included in the budgets to cover expenses incurred in preparation for the meetings "such as printing programs, ballots for commissioner, tickets, badges, etc." The item was dropped from the 1958–59 budget, however, and thereafter everything had to be paid for out of registration receipts; thus it was important to shop around for the best bargains available in the way of convention facilities and services and at the same time to put together a program that would motivate Mississippi's lawyers to attend and to bring their spouses with them. President Hugh Clayton announced two innovations in 1960. Instead of single speeches on various topics, there were to be discussion panels presided over by judges. The annual banquet was to be made the occasion for bringing in various persons who had "done things" for the State Bar during the preceding year, especially legislators, and thanking them officially for their good work. It was also at the 1960 meeting that the practice was begun, in imitation of A.B.A. annual meetings, of referring to full sessions as "general assemblies."

The 1966 annual meeting, the last but one to be held in Jackson, took place in the Heidelberg Hotel beginning on Thursday, June 16, and running through Saturday, the 18th.[11] and its program was a typical one for the 1960s.

At noon on Thursday the officers and directors of the Junior Bar Section met for lunch in one room, and the Board of Bar Commissioners lunched in another. Then at 2:00 P.M. the Junior Bar held its annual meeting, and the Circuit Judges Conference met. That

10. The Clayton amendment, as further amended, was formally adopted at the 1963 meeting. In 1967 article V was reworded yet again, leaving out all reference to 1965.

11. The program may be seen in the State Archives at Jackson.

evening at seven the Junior Bar hosted a reception followed by a buffet dinner.

Friday began early for the fellows of the Bar Foundation, who assembled at eight for their annual breakfast meeting. The first general assembly began at nine with the usual opening ceremonies and speeches of welcome, followed by Orma R. Smith's presidential address. At ten the first panel discussion began, presided over by Judge N. S. ("Soggy") Sweat, Jr., who, as chairman of the program committee for the meeting, had been responsible for putting it together. The topic was "Recent Developments in the Law," and the discussion was started off by the chief justice of the state's Supreme Court, W. N. Ethridge, Jr., who talked on "Developments in Procedural Law." John W. Wade, who after serving for several years on the University of Mississippi law faculty had gone on to become dean of the law school at Vanderbilt, then spoke on "Developments in Tort Law." The third speaker was a circuit judge from Florida, John A. Murphree, who talked on "Our State Courts —Developments in Judicial Administration." A final half-hour was devoted to questions and answers before the discussion ended at noon.

Members apparently had to find their own lunch; then, beginning at two, a second panel discussion was held on the topic "Should we adopt for our state courts rules of practice and procedures in line with the federal rules?" At six-fifteen in the evening President Smith hosted a reception, which was followed by the annual banquet at seven-thirty. The featured speaker at the banquet was Dr. Charles Jarvis, distinguished citizen of San Marcos, Texas. After the meal had been eaten and all of the speeches made, members and their guests moved on to the annual dance at half-past nine.

At eight on Saturday morning the past presidents got together for breakfast, presumably in order to decide whom to nominate as president-elect for the coming year. Another business breakfast was held at the same time by the members of the Mississippi Conference of Judges. The second general assembly was called to order by the president at nine-thirty. After Dean Joshua Morse III had spoken on what the University Law School was currently doing to provide "Legal Education for the Student and the Practitioner" and on some of its plans for the future, the chairmen of the various committees presented their reports for the past year. The resolutions proposed by the Resolutions Committee were all passed with only one amendment, and Hugh Clayton was elected to represent the Mississippi State Bar in the House of Delegates of the A.B.A. Then Hugh Clayton nominated N. W. Overstreet, Jr. of Jackson for the office of president-elect, and "Mr. Overstreet was elected by acclamation."

In accordance with custom B. B. McLendon, Jr. of Jackson, outgoing president of the Junior Bar Section, next was elected second vice-president by acclamation. Then Orma R. Smith introduced the incoming president, John T. Armstrong. After the nineteen districts had each announced their choice for commissioner, the "Sixty-First Annual Convention of the Mississippi State Bar adjourned *sine die*."

While the business of the Bar was thus being taken care of that morning by the members, those wives who had accompanied their husbands to Jackson but were not themselves lawyers were on a bus tour which marked the culmination of a whole schedule of "ladies' activities" that had been provided during the three days of the meeting. On Thursday afternoon, from three-thirty to five, there had been a pool-patio party at the Sun 'n' Sand Motel. The ladies' program on Friday had commenced at ten in the morning with a private tour of the antebellum Governor's Mansion. From there they had gone out to the Jackson Country Club for a reception at eleven-thirty followed by a gala luncheon and style show with door-prizes. Meanwhile the hospitality room at the Heidelberg remained open through each day, serving coffee, cakes, and doughnuts and providing everything necessary for bridge games. It had all been organized by the ladies' activities committee of the Hinds County Lawyers' Wives' Auxiliary, whose members acted as hostesses. In the evenings, of course, they and their out-of-town visitors had attended the various scheduled social events with their husbands and friends.

By the mid-1970s some changes had been made in the typical program, but it remained essentially the same. In 1973 at the Broadwater Beach Hotel in Biloxi, things got underway with a golf tournament on Wednesday afternoon, followed by an "early arrivals" cocktail party in the evening. On Thursday morning the Board of Commissioners met, and the Young Lawyers met in the afternoon. Another cocktail party that evening was followed by a "seafood safari." On Friday morning and afternoon and on Saturday morning, as in 1966, business sessions were held. And the president's reception was again held on Friday evening, followed by the annual dinner and then the annual dance.

Beginning in 1975 the Board of Commissioners began holding a breakfast meeting on the first morning, followed by the annual meeting of the Young Lawyers, who thus at last had a whole day for their deliberations as Phil Stone had suggested.[12] General assemblies were held on the second and third mornings, while the second afternoon was left free for recreational activities and small group meetings. Perhaps because the popular dances of the mid-1970s were somewhat too strenuous to engage in at the end of a long day of meetings, sports and games, feasting and drinking, the long-established institution of the annual dance, or, as it was called prior to World War II, the "annual ball," was done away with in favor of sitting and listening to live "entertainment."

An observer cannot help being struck by how much most of the entertainment provided at annual meetings by the mid-1960s and early 70s differed from that which the members of the Mississippi Bar had enjoyed back in the interwar years at meetings held in towns such as Greenwood, Laurel, Clarksdale, or Meridian. Such "down home-plain folks" amusements as horseshoe pitching and softball contests, movies, country club barbecues, and amateur

---

12. In 1975 the meeting ran from Sunday through Wednesday; but for 1976 and 1977 there was a return to the usual Wednesday through Saturday schedule.

concerts three decades later had lost their appeal for the sophisticated members of one of the *élite* professions in an increasingly prosperous "sunbelt" state. They enjoyed instead golf and tennis tournaments, fashion shows, exotic foods, and professional entertainers. Perhaps the amount of pleasure derived was no greater, but the change was certainly remarkable.

Another notable change, of course, had occurred with regard to the liquor laws and their enforcement. In the 1920s and 30s, as we have noted, welcoming speeches at the opening ceremonies of the annual meetings nearly always contained broad hints that bootleg whiskey would be readily available for all those who wanted it, coupled with firm assurances that local law officers had orders not to bother roystering attorneys in their revels. But at the 1972 annual meeting the president of the Harrison County Bar Association warned his colleagues: "The Bar Association does not enjoy immunity from arrest from the Biloxi Police Department, so I would caution you to drive your automobile carefully . . . especially when leaving a bar." Liquor had become legal in many Mississippi cities, with the paradoxical result that the liquor laws and the laws against public drunkenness were being much more strictly applied.

Members of the State Bar, the record shows, had played a major role in bringing the change about. As the Second World War was drawing to a close, Bidwell Adam, in his presidential address to the 1945 annual meeting, had denounced the statute passed by the 1944 session of the Legislature imposing a state tax on bootleg liquor.[13] The measure was actually entitled, "An act to discourage black markets by imposing a tax equal to ten per cent of the gross proceeds of sales . . . of any tangible property, articles or commodities whatsoever, the sale . . . of which is prohibited by law," but its true intent was clearly revealed by the fact that it was listed in the index to the laws of 1944 under the heading of "Beer and Wine" but not under "Gasoline" or any of the other usual black market commodities of the World War II era. "It is my honest belief," Adam said, "that the black-market tax . . . is a disgrace to the fair

13. *Miss. Laws* (1944), c. 139.

name of Mississippi. . . . We should either break up this disgraceful form of racketeering and legalize the sale of whiskey, or confess our lack of courage to handle the situation."

No action was taken that year. Actually, it was not until 1950, when the Junior Bar Section proposed that the State Bar "take a stand on the repeal of the Prohibition Laws in Mississippi," that the State Bar faced the question, and they were not prepared to be quite that firm quite that fast. After "a very lengthy discussion," the matter was "referred to the Commissioners for consideration." In 1951 the Junior Bar brought the matter up again by suggesting two resolutions. The first stated "that it is the consensus of the Mississippi State Bar that it favors laws which would legalize the sale of alcoholic liquors in the state" and "that the Bar shall implement the views so expressed . . . by sponsoring an educational program on the issues involved." The second called for the repeal of "the Black Market Tax" on liquor because it lowered respect for law enforcement and because it brought ridicule on the state. Evidently in a more aggressive mood than they had been the year before, the Bar passed the second of the two resolutions and added to it a further recommendation that the Legislature "repeal the present asinine, unenforceable, and hypocritical prohibition law."

The Legislature was totally unresponsive, however, and the matter was forgotten for more than a decade at State Bar meetings. But by 1965 Governor Paul B. Johnson, Jr., a member of the Jackson Bar, was taking the stance that the liquor laws should be either enforced or repealed. And the State Bar at its meeting in Biloxi that year passed a resolution expressing the same point of view. The preamble to the resolution stated that Mississippi was "known throughout the Nation as the most law-abiding of the several states,"[14] that its people "have always believed in and have been exponents of self-government," that the prohibition of liquor in some counties and towns was "decidedly contrary to the will of the

14. Actually, according to the F.B.I. report on *Crime in the United States* (1964–65), in 1964 Mississippi had only the fifth-lowest crime rate in proportion to her population, behind New Hampshire, North Dakota, Vermont, and West Virginia.

local people," that the prohibition laws "were generally and consistently ignored," and that by taxing the sale of illegal liquor the state placed itself in an "inconsistent position" and a "hypocritical situation." They, therefore, called upon the Legislature

> either to take such steps as [were] necessary in order to fully and completely enforce the prohibition laws uniformly and consistently in each of the several counties of the State, or [else] to pass such legislation as may be necessary in order to permit the several counties . . . by vote of their people to remove their counties from the chaotic conditions which now exist and to place them under some reasonable type of regulated sale of intoxicating liquors.

The 1966 session of the Legislature finally did respond by passing House Bill number 112, which allowed the sale and possession of liquor in towns or counties on a local option basis, and created the Alcoholic Beverage Commission to regulate sales and enforce the new laws.[15] The battle had been won.

The Junior Bar Section, which had spearheaded the first attack against the state's unenforced and hypocritical liquor laws, continued through the 1950s, 60s, and early 70s to be the most energetic and active group within the State Bar and the main originator of new ideas and programs. It brought in interesting speakers to address its annual sessions, including, in 1952, Erle Stanley Gardner, the California lawyer and creator of America's best-known, though fictional, criminal defense attorney, Perry Mason, and, in 1962, Leon Jaworski of Texas, who still had more than a decade to go before he would become famous as the second Watergate "Special Prosecutor." A survey of their meeting reports indicates that they continued to be especially interested in admissions to the Bar, continuing legal education, and preventing the unauthorized practice of the law by court clerks, real estate agents, justices of the peace, and others. By the 1970s drug abuse, prison conditions, and mental institutions had been added to their concerns. In 1964 they

15. *Miss. Laws* (1966), c. 540. This bill was reassuringly entitled "AN ACT declaring the policy of this state as fostering, encouraging and vigorously enforcing the prohibition laws. . . ."

voted their unanimous disapproval of a suggestion that the Junior Bar Conference of the A.B.A. be renamed the "Young Lawyers Conference." But the national group made the change anyway, and so in 1970 they followed suit, voting to change their name to the "Young Lawyers Section" of the Mississippi State Bar.

It was also from the Junior Bar that the initiative came for the creation of a monthly periodical named the *Mississippi Lawyer*, which began publication in August, 1954, under the editorship of two young Jackson lawyers, Byron Thomas Hetrick and John C. Sullivan, Jr. The secretarial work involved in putting the publication together and getting it out, like every other kind of paperwork involved with the Bar at that time, was handled by Mrs. Nevels and her staff. Essentially a news-sheet, the new periodical printed news and information useful and interesting to members of the State Bar and thus provided a valuable supplement to the more formal, scholarly, and technical material published in the *Law Journal*.

The *Law Journal* itself, receiving from four to five thousand dollars from the State Bar in the 1950s and half as much again in the 1960s, by 1952 was publishing regularly four issues a year in December, March, May, and October. The October issue was always made up of the proceedings of the annual meeting the previous June, together with a Bar Directory organized alphabetically by cities. Instead of being included in the proceedings, the committee reports were printed in a separate appendix, and the proceedings themselves contained only a brief summary of the business conducted in each session and the texts of the major speeches.

That, of course, is frustrating for the historian, and by 1957–58 complaints were even coming in from some members of the Bar that too much was being edited out and that the full texts were not being provided of the materials that were published. In response the *Law Journal* Board and the editors replied that they were only conforming with what by then was a long-established practice and that to have published just the committee reports for 1957 "without the exercise of editorial license" would have required seventy-six more pages and cost another eight hundred dollars. So a compromise was reached whereby, beginning with the October, 1958, issue, a committee consisting of the president of the State Bar, the chairman of the *Law Journal* Board, the faculty advisor, and the editor would directly oversee what was printed and what was left out. That apparently worked well for a while, but by 1968 most committee reports were being published elsewhere and by 1969 those speeches that were published were considerably abridged. In 1971, apart from the Bar Directory, fewer than half the pages in the October issue were devoted to the State Bar's proceedings. In 1972 and subsequent years the proceedings were not published at all.

The cost of printing even a single page had risen sharply. There are so many legal issues and questions that a good law journal must devote space to and so many books to be reviewed that most State Bars do not have their proceedings published. Nevertheless, some lawyers in the state have been unhappy about the situation and a compromise may have to be worked out.[16]

Besides reading the *Mississippi Lawyer* and studying the *Law Journal* during the past twenty-five years, most attorneys in the state have had another point of contact with the State Bar through their local bar associations. Before, during, and immediately after World War II, however, those local associations that did exist had been more or less left to themselves. After the attempt during the 1920s to strengthen the voluntary Bar Association by building up a network of affiliated local groups had failed, the leadership of the State Bar had concentrated on operating on a statewide basis while the existing local bars reciprocated by showing little interest in the State Bar. President Snow told the annual meeting in 1953 that one reason he had hesitated to take on the presidency the year before was that he had feared it would entail a great deal of travelling around the state talking to local bar groups. In fact, however, he need not have worried because as he said, "As President of the State Bar Association I received only one invitation throughout the

16. Historians can take comfort in the fact that complete stenographic records of the modern proceedings are made, and they are kept in the State Bar office in Jackson.

year to attend a meeting of a local bar association away from Jackson," a meeting of the Tri-County Bar at Brookhaven.

Evidently he got his message across because President Jerome S. Hafter reported to the 1954 meeting that he had been overwhelmed with more invitations to attend county and district bar meetings than he could possibly find the time to accept. By 1956 there was in existence a State Bar Committee on "Coordination of Bar Activities," and it organized the first "Conference of Local Bar Associations," which met at Jackson on June 21, the day prior to the opening of the 1956 annual meeting. The delegates, drawn from every part of the state, adopted a constitution and by-laws, elected Betty B. Tucker of Jackson their president, and chose three vice-presidents, one each from northern, central, and southern Mississippi. Mrs. Nevels, of course, was to serve as secretary and treasurer. Six standing committees were to be set up on Membership, Programs, Public Relations, Legislation, Professional Ethics, and Professional Fees; the president, vice-presidents, and committee chairmen, together with the presidents of the local bar associations, the president of the State Bar, and the secretary, were to constitute a board of directors which would meet in April and August every year.

During the year 1956–57 a total of nine district bar conferences were held, each of which was well attended by lawyers and their wives, and a *Handbook for Local Bar Associations* was prepared and distributed. In a report to the 1957 annual meeting, which was approved by the membership, the Committee on Coordination of Bar Activities recommended that the State Bar prepare and carry out an overall program of activities conducted through local bar associations with the aim of helping lawyers everywhere in the state to keep "abreast of the studies and findings of the Mississippi State Bar and the American Bar Association. . . ." Noting the enthusiasm that lawyers' wives had shown for attending the district bar meetings, the committee also recommended that ladies' auxiliary organizations be established at the local and state level, and many local bars did soon organize ladies' groups.

Ten years later, in 1967, there were fifty-three local bar associations in Mississippi, and sixty-seven of the eighty-two counties either had their own association or else had grouped together with the bars of a number of neighboring counties to form one. De Soto County and the cities of Jackson and Gulfport also had local junior bar groups. By the end of 1976 only some half-dozen, thinly-populated counties neither had their own local bar nor were included in one that covered a wider area, and the number of local junior bars had risen to ten. As one might expect, the most active local groups were to be found in such urban or suburban areas as De Soto County, Lee County, Hinds County, Warren County, Lauderdale County, and Harrison County. The total number of local bar associations in Mississsippi in the Bicentennial Year was seventy-one.[17]

One of several useful functions that local bar associations could perform, the 1957 committee report had noted, was carrying out public relations work for the legal profession at the grass roots level, and the Public Relations Committee in its report for the same year emphasized the help it had received from local bars in putting on the air television and radio shows entitled "You and the Law." The Forrest County Bar Association had been responsible for initiating the first such series of broadcasts on WFOR in Hattiesburg in 1952. Other groups had circulated pamphlets or else had newspaper releases printed getting the lawyers' point of view across and informing the public as to how to obtain the best in legal advice and services.

The Public Relations Committee in 1957 had two major recommendations to make. One was that the name "Mississippi State Bar" be changed as soon as possible to "Mississippi Bar Association" in order to emphasize both the relationship with the American Bar Association and the relationship with other state bars, most of which were called bar associations. Its other recommendation was that the chairman of its committee be given the title of "Director of Public Relations of the Mississippi State Bar." Both recommendations were approved by the annual meeting. As things turned out, however, the first was never implemented. The com-

17. The information is derived from Mississippi State Bar lists.

mittee itself continued to refer to the "Mississippi State Bar" in its subsequent reports. With regard to the second, from 1960 through 1963 Gene A. Wilkinson of Jackson was listed as "Public Relations Director" among the officers of the State Bar immediately after the second vice-president and ahead of the secretary-treasurer. In 1964, however, the title was dropped.

Public relations of a particular kind, working for a better understanding among both lawyers and laymen of what the law is, its history, and its philosophy, was to be one of the functions of the Mississippi Bar Foundation which was established with the encouragement of the Mississippi State Bar in 1962–63 during the presidency of C. Sidney Carleton. Twelve years earlier Phil Stone had suggested the creation of an endowment fund to "promote the interests of the lawyers of Mississippi." Modelled on the already-existing American Bar Foundation, the new organization aimed at doing what Stone had suggested and more. The original plan for it was drawn up by a six-man committee, chaired by N. W. Overstreet, Jr., that was appointed by Carleton in the summer of 1962. On December 6 of that year their recommendations were approved by the Board of Commissioners, and on December 11 the new corporation they had designed received a charter from the State of Mississippi. On January 25, 1963, the committee members and the Bar Commissioners, functioning as the incorporators, met and adopted a charter, enacted a set of by-laws, and elected the first five-man board of trustees. On February 13, 1963, the trustees held their first meeting and elected W. S. Henley to be the first president, N. W. Overstreet, Jr. to be the first vice-president, and Alice Nevels to be the first secretary-treasurer.

The purpose of the new body was explained by Supreme Court Justice W. N. Ethridge, Jr. in an article which appeared in the May, 1963, issue of the *Law Journal*. Like its A.B.A. prototype, he explained, its general aim would be "to help close the gap by increasing our professional reach without surrendering the values which have brought us the long distance we have already come." More specifically, its members would work (1) to improve and facilitate the administration of justice; (2) to promote legal study, research, and teaching; (3) to publish and distribute literary works on legal subjects; and (4) to acquire, preserve, and exhibit rare documents, books, and other items connected with the history of law and justice. Members of the Mississippi Bar in good standing could apply for election as fellows of the foundation. If elected, they would be expected to pay dues of $50 per year for five years, after which they would become life members with no further financial obligations in what was intended to be "a fraternal group of distinguished members of the profession. . . ."[18]

Among other projects during its first fifteen years, the Foundation published a history of the nineteenth-century Mississippi Bar Associations (1966) and a history of the state Supreme Court from 1817 to 1948 (1973). In 1974 it began providing financial backing for a course on "The Legal Profession," which is required to be taken by all University of Mississippi Law School students and which brings in as guest lecturers the officers of the Bar and other distinguished attorneys from around the state to talk on problems of legal practice and questions of legal ethics. Thus a program which had its beginnings in 1922 when President Leftwich twice travelled to Oxford at Dean Kimbrough's invitation to lecture to the students on legal ethics was finally brought to full fruition.

The idea for the Foundation was but one of several which the Mississippi State Bar derived from the A.B.A., with which it has always had a very close relationship. Through the 1940s it had continued to be the custom to elect the outgoing president as the Mississippi delegate to the A.B.A. House of Delegates, but in 1949, in order better to conform to the A.B.A. constitution, it was resolved that delegates in the future should be elected for two-year terms with the serving president of the State Bar each year acting as alternate if the elected delegate for any reason could not attend the national group's annual meeting. Usually the delegates elected have been recent past presidents, men familiar with the workings of the organized State Bar in Mississippi and with the issues that concern it.

---

18. XXXIV (1962–63), 244–302.

VII

The Recent Past—The Issues

1952–1976

Of all the prominent lawyers who have served as president of the Mississippi State Bar since World War II, his contemporaries seem to agree that the most outstanding has been John C. Satterfield, now of Yazoo City, who held the office from 1955 to 1956. Satterfield throughout his career had always been an active A.B.A. member, and no doubt was mainly responsible for the fact that in the A.B.A.'s 1956 membership drive Mississippi exceeded its quota of 342 new members.[1]

By the time of the 1958 annual meeting in Biloxi, there was already talk that Satterfield would soon be president of the A.B.A., and the members of the Mississippi Bar voted consistently to support his candidacy. In fact, he was narrowly defeated at Los Angeles in 1958 and again in 1959 at Miami. In 1960 at Washington, D.C., he finally was chosen as the A.B.A.'s president-elect. Back at Biloxi in June, 1961, he gave an address on "What Can Bar Associations Do for Lawyers?" and urged his Mississippi colleagues to join him at the upcoming A.B.A. annual meeting in St. Louis for his inauguration as their state's first chief executive of the eighty-three-year-old organization to which some 100,000 of the nation's 236,000 lawyers belonged.

Back home again a year later, in 1962, he reminisced happily about the twenty-two foreign countries and forty-two American states he had visited first as the A.B.A.'s president-elect and then as its president. He also apparently thought it necessary to reas-

1. *Miss. LJ*, XXVII (1955–56), 321.

sure his listeners that, in spite of what they might think, "throughout the United States there is not any prejudice against Mississippi or the South." Perhaps there was no prejudice in 1962, but relations with the A.B.A. and with members of the legal profession in other parts of the country were to become somewhat strained in the years that immediately followed.

The problem was an old one of race relations which had periodically plagued Mississippi for a century. Very little had resulted from President Truman's Civil Rights Commission, and during the early 1950s things remained for the most part as they had been. But then a new voice spoke out on the subject of black and white, one that lawyers were accustomed to listen to with the greatest respect, the United States Supreme Court. Presided over by President Eisenhower's new appointee, Chief Justice Earl Warren of California, the Court, on May 7, 1954, ruled unanimously in *Brown* v. *Board of Education* that the Equal Protection clause of the Fourteenth Amendment was violated by the existence of a racially segregated public school system. The doctrine of "separate but equal," enunciated by the Court in *Plessy* v. *Ferguson* (1896), was no longer to be the law of the land. Most Mississippi lawyers, like most Mississippi whites, could not bring themselves to believe that equality under the law necessarily entailed integration. In his presidential address to the 1954 annual meeting, Jerome S. Hafter forecast that the *Brown* decision would "for many years to come aggravate the racial condition in our state and . . . set progress back many years."

In Hafter's opinion the justices had been primarily influenced "by newspapers, periodicals and pressure groups which have permeated the press." Such groups "argued that it is better to change our way of life in the South if by doing so our diplomats can say to the colored nations of the world that we welcome them as our allies and consider them as our social equals." He believed that "had the present Court been composed of experienced judges promoted from the federal bench or from the supreme court judges of the various states" instead of men "whose appointments in some respects may be considered political," then "the opinion would have been based on more legal and judicial reasoning." It would require the efforts of the best legal minds in the South combined and united, he said, to work out a satisfactory solution.

The Legislature, meanwhile, had already established a Legal Education Advisory Committee consisting of twenty-five members including the governor, the lieutenant governor, the speaker of the House of Representatives, the chief justice, and the president of the State Bar to advise them in the crisis. Before adjourning, the members of the Bar voted to offer the committee their "advice, interest, support and assistance to the end that justice may be promoted, public tranquillity and harmony maintained and the best interests of the citizens and school children of both races may be served and safeguarded."

A year later Dean Robert J. Farley in his presidential address to the 1955 meeting reported on the work of the Advisory Committee. There had been "conflicting ideas and heated debates," he said, but all of the members had been "patriotically bent on doing what each considered best for our state."

In 1955–56 the Bar's own Committee on the Maintenance of Constitutional Rights of the States and of Individuals considered the whole issue. Hugh Clayton presented its report to the 1956 meeting where it was approved by a vote of the members. If the trend in constitutional interpretation being followed by the Warren Court continued, it warned, "the United States may soon reach the point of no return, at which a strong centralized and socialistic government becomes the master and not the servant of the states and the people." Specifically it stated the belief "that lawyers are justified in opposing recent decisions of the Court which are in conflict with long established judicial precedent," and it lauded the Legislature for its adoption on February 29, 1956, of the "Interposition Resolution" which stated in part that *Brown* and several other recent Supreme Court decisions were "in violation of the Constitutions of the United States and of the State of Mississippi, and are therefore unconstitutional and of no lawful effect within the territorial limits of the State of Mississippi."[2] The committee made a similar report in 1957 which was also approved, and that year the Citizenship Committee recommended that in the citizenship program in the state's high schools "continued emphasis be made of our stand on segregation of the races and why we believe that same should be maintained; and further, why we believe that it is to the best interest of both races to continue segregation in all phases of the State's life. . . ."

Meanwhile, Mississippi's schools remained totally segregated, and *Brown* in fact had very little real impact on the state in the later 1950s. In its second *Brown* decision, handed down on May 31, 1955, the Supreme Court had said that states were to integrate their school systems "with all deliberate speed." That old English chancery law phrase meant different things to different people in the twentieth-century United States, however, and, furthermore, the desegregation of the schools in every state required a separate lawsuit if the state chose to ignore *Brown.* Even where a lawsuit was fought and won, there still remained the problem of enforcing it. The year 1957 might be regarded as a pivotal one because it was the year that the civil rights division of the Justice Department was founded, and in September President Eisenhower used federal troops to enforce integration of the public schools in Little Rock, Arkansas.

Even then five more years were to elapse before federal troops were used in Mississippi. But finally, on the last night of September, 1962, President Kennedy sent several thousand U.S. soldiers onto the campus of the University of Mississippi to enforce the court order mandating the enrollment of black Air Force veteran James Meredith as an "Ole Miss" undergraduate. Then in the summer of 1963 "freedom riders" travelled through the state by bus, integrating public facilities and appealing to the protection of the law when their efforts were resisted. The Civil Rights Act of 1964 made any such resistance no longer merely a tort but a federal crime. During the "long hot summer" of that year the attention of

---

2. *Miss. Laws* (1956), c. 466.

the nation was focused on Mississippi as a massive drive, coordinated by the Council of Federated Organizations (COFO), was carried out, mostly by student "civil rights workers" from northern states, to assist blacks to assert their legal rights, particularly the right to register to vote. The discovery of the bodies of three murdered civil rights workers on August 4, near Philadelphia in Neshoba County, caused many outsiders to regard the Magnolia State with loathing as a land of violent lawlessness and terror.

It was all very distressing to the members of the Mississippi State Bar. Most of them believed in the rightfulness of racial segregation; all of them believed, because they were lawyers, in the rule of law. On June 19, 1963, the annual meeting for that year got underway in Jackson. At the same time in Washington, D.C., President Kennedy was hosting a White House conference on civil rights problems at which the Mississippi Bar was represented by its former president, Sherwood W. Wise; he had agreed to go in place of President Carleton, who, of course, had to be in Jackson. In the Mississippi Capitol the members passed a resolution calling on Wise to inform the White House group that, while they supported "the cause of constitutional government and the orderly and fair administration of justice," they could not approve or support "the present unwarranted invasions of the reserved powers of the several states" which they believed constituted "a serious threat to the freedom of the individual citizens of this nation." Another resolution passed a year later at the 1964 meeting, just as COFO's "freedom summer" was beginning, condemned "deliberate acts of lawlessness which are calculated to provoke arrest" and "the exportation of agitators, professional or otherwise, by any organization or group, to other communities or states for the deliberate purpose of inciting violence, riot and arrest." At the same time they asserted their firm support of "the right of any individual who or group which feels aggrieved to freely and peaceably discuss and resolve such grievances, and present them to the public authorities for redress" and, if redress were not provided, of their "right to seek to rectify their alleged wrongs in the courts."

Two weeks later President Lyndon Johnson's signing of the

Civil Rights Act greatly expanded the legal rights that the courts were to protect. But when civil rights workers and Mississippi blacks co-operating with them went to court "to rectify their alleged wrongs," who would represent them? There were only three black attorneys residing in the state in the early sixties.[3] White Mississippi attorneys who took on "outside agitators" or "uppity" blacks as clients were apt to come under intolerable pressure from their friends, neighbors, and other clients. There was also the question of who was to pay the fees and cover the expenses involved, for the United States Supreme Court had just declared in the landmark case of *Gideon* v. *Wainwright* (1963) that state courts must furnish counsel for indigent defendants. If attorneys came from outside the state to handle civil rights cases what was to be their relationship to the Mississippi State Bar?

In his presidential address to the 1965 annual meeting at Biloxi, Earl T. Thomas told how, at the outset of his term the previous summer, he had been confronted by "the problems spawned by the tornado twins of *Gideon* v. *Wainwright* and the 'Mississippi Summer Project.'" On July 15, 1964, a "Special Liaison Committee" consisting of 322 members of the State Bar had been formed to provide attorneys for those who sought legal assistance but could not otherwise obtain it. News releases had been sent out to the media around the state emphasizing the duty of lawyers to defend the indigent and the unpopular. But most civil rights campaigners did not trust Mississippi lawyers. They wanted to bring in their own. So in August, 1964, COFO had filed a suit in the federal court in Jackson, in which President Thomas and Executive Director Nevels were named as defendants, and which sought an injunction prohibiting the enforcement of the Unified Bar Act and other state statutes regulating the practice of law with regard to lawyers engaged in civil rights cases. Happily, Thomas reported, on June 12, 1965, Judge Harold Cox had non-suited the plaintiffs.

By that time, however, three outside groups of lawyers had

3. Francis B. Stevens and John L. Maxey II, "Representing the Unrepresented," *Miss. LJ*, XLIV (1973), 339.

come in to handle civil rights cases in the state; all of them located their offices on Farish Street in Jackson. One was the NAACP's Legal Defense and Education Fund, Incorporated. A second was the Lawyer's Constitutional Defense Committee (LCDC), which derived its backing from such groups as the National Council of Churches, the American Civil Liberties Union, the American Jewish Congress, and Martin Luther King's Southern Christian Leadership Conference. The third was the Lawyer's Committee for Civil Rights Under Law (LCCRUL), which had developed out of the 1963 White House conference on civil rights and was backed by the A.B.A.

Of the three groups only the LCCRUL ever had any sort of relationship with the Mississippi State Bar. Before its Jackson office was opened in June, 1965, consultations had taken place between members of the Committee and State Bar officials; on May 24 the Board of Bar Commissioners had passed a resolution pledging their co-operation on the understanding that the attorneys working for the Committee would all be highly qualified and would only represent clients who could clearly prove that they could not obtain legal representation from a member of the State Bar because of inability to pay or for some other valid reason. A.B.A. president-elect Orison S. Marden of New York City told the 1965 annual meeting how delighted the national organization was with the "most heartening" attitude taken by the state group towards LCCRUL.

For about a year all went well. A fairly close liaison was maintained between the Committee's Jackson office staff and the officers of the State Bar. By the latter part of 1966, however, the "good though not intimate relationship" had broken down. By that time LCCRUL's lawyers in Mississippi, like those representing the other two "Farish Street" groups, were no longer content merely to provide representation for defendants charged with civil rights-related crimes. More and more they were engaging in "affirmative action" litigation which was aimed, according to one nationally circulated report, at "changing the entire structure of justice and law enforcement in the South." After a complaint to the Committee's Washington office had only resulted in a "partisan, defensive and unsatisfactory response," President Armstrong told the 1967 annual meeting, the Commissioners had voted on April 7 to repeal their endorsement of the project and end their co-operation with its officials.

In spite of several attempts on both sides during the next two years, the breach was never healed. But time passed on, and race relations and civil rights became problems in the North as well as in the old Confederacy. At the 1969 annual meeting in Jackson, A.B.A. president-elect Bernard Segal of Philadelphia, Pennsylvania, reported that that year two-thirds of LCCRUL's budget was being spent on its Urban Areas Program in fourteen cities, all of which, except for Atlanta, were outside the South. And he noted with pleasure that the Mississippi State Bar's Commissioners had recently approved a program aimed at providing legal aid in cases involving "civil rights including criminal matters wherein an alleged denial of civil rights constitutes a portion of the defense, as well as in cases wherein the client seeks affirmative relief to establish civil rights."

The provision of legal assistance for those unable to provide it for themselves was not, of course, a totally new idea in Mississippi in the 1960s. During World War II, as we have seen, it had been made available to servicemen through the Legal Assistance Program. In 1950 R. W. Thompson in his presidential address had suggested that "Legal Aid" or a "Lawyer Reference" plan ought to be provided for the less well-to-do because otherwise the legal profession in America might one day be socialized just like the medical profession had recently been in Britain. But the first actual step was taken by the Junior Bar Section in 1952 when it sponsored a Legal Aid Society for Hinds County. At the 1960 annual meeting it was reported that the Society had handled 341 cases in 1959. Then, in 1963, the United States Supreme Court's *Gideon* decision made it even more imperative that some sort of statewide plan be developed, but for the next three years the whole issue was complicated by the controversy over the outside groups of lawyers who had come into the state.

By 1966, however, one committee of the Bar had drafted a Public Defender statute for submission to the Legislature, and another was at work studying the whole question of legal aid to the poor. In June President Smith warned the annual meeting that the recently-created Office of Economic Opportunity (OEO), as part of President Johnson's "War on Poverty," was getting ready to put a lot of money into the state for legal assistance projects and that, if the State Bar did not itself come up with an acceptance program, "we are going to find other groups taking over and running the project staffed with lawyers brought into Mississippi for the purpose."

The Bar's draft of a Public Defender act, though rejected by the 1966 session of the Legislature, was eventually passed in the calmer political atmosphere of 1971. Providing for the first time a fair and realistic fee schedule for the assigned attorney, it benefited both the members of the legal profession and indigent defendants.[4] But the plan for a legal aid program approved by the 1967 annual meeting, with the provisos that the Mississippi State Bar must retain complete control over every aspect of the program and the client must have a completely free choice as to what lawyer represented him, was never accepted by OEO officials in Washington in spite of Segal's commendation. Instead the Legal Services unit of OEO continued to support North Mississippi Rural Legal Services (NMRLS), which they had originally funded in April, 1966. Staffed at first by members of the University of Mississippi Law School faculty, NMRLS was intended to combine legal services for the poor with a teaching program for law students. However, an increasing emphasis on class action litigation, in which state and local agencies were frequently the defendants, made the program so controversial that the University judged it prudent to end its sponsorship in 1968. Thereafter NMRLS was funded through Mary Holmes College, a predominantly black, private institution. OEO also funded in 1966 Coahoma Legal Aid, Incorporated (CLA) through the Community Action Program in Coahoma County.

4. *Miss. Laws* (1971), c. 490. See also Parham H. Williams and William M. Bost, Jr., "The Assigned Counsel System: An Exercise of Servitude," *Miss. LJ*, XLII (1970), 32–59.

And, in 1971, over the objections of both the State Bar and the Hinds County Bar Association, OEO not only re-funded NMRLS but also provided funds for a new project called Jackson Hinds Community Legal Services (CLS).[5] By 1976 NMRLS, CLA, and CLS still had no formal relationship with the State Bar, but all of their boards of directors did include State Bar members and they were tending to employ mostly Mississippi lawyers of both races and both sexes.

The Mississippi State Bar, meanwhile, had administered one highly successful legal aid program that it could look back on with pride. Immediately following the Hurricane Camille disaster in August, 1969, an emergency grant of $50,000 had been obtained from OEO. The money was used to equip and run a camper vehicle which served as a mobile law office for those who urgently needed assistance in putting their affairs back in order in the stricken counties. Over thirty lawyers volunteered their services for the program from all around the state, while at the same time the local bar associations in Jackson, Stone, and Pearl River counties operated their own supplementary aid programs as did also the South Central Bar Association consisting of lawyers from Perry, Forest, and Lamar counties.

Through all of these cataclysmic events and revolutionary changes and developments, Mississippi's lawyers still had to keep themselves up to date on what was happening in every aspect of the practice of law. The State Bar was their principal means for doing so, especially through its committees. In 1935 there had only been half a dozen committees at work, but after World War II, and especially in the fifties, a period of proliferation began. Five new committees were established in 1951. In 1957 an Atomic Energy Committee was set up, which reported to the 1958 annual meeting that, with regard to possible nuclear accidents, "as far as theories of liability are concerned, it is our best judgment that the common law of negligence is adequate." In 1962 a "Long Range

5. Stevens and Maxey, pp. 344–46.

Planning Committee" was added to the list, which totalled forty-eight by 1963. That was the peak year; by 1966 the number of committees was reduced to forty. President Curtis told the 1969 meeting that he had reduced it to thirty-five, which still may have been too many. His successors continued the trend, however, so that by the end of 1976 there were only twenty-six committees on the list.[6] Meanwhile, in addition to all of the matters being studied by the various committees, the increasing popularity of air travel meant that a much greater variety of speakers could be invited to address the annual meetings on a wider range of topics. The guest speaker at the annual dinner in 1969 was astronaut Don Lind.[7]

In a rapidly developing state and a fast-changing world, Mississippi lawyers after World War II found they could no longer depend throughout all of their professional careers on what they had learned while in law school. The first annual Mississippi Law Institute was held in Jackson in 1946 to assist lawyers returning from the services to civilian practice. Held in mid-winter, the Institutes were sponsored by the Junior Bar Section and came to serve almost the function of mid-annual meetings of the State Bar. Two hundred fifty lawyers attended the Institute held at Jackson on December 5 and 6, 1958, to hear a program offered by the nationally famous California trial lawyer Melvin M. Belli and his associates on trial problems, practices, and procedures. And another famous Californian, Erle Stanley Gardner, was back again as the banquet speaker. Three months earlier, on September 5 and 6, in the Millsaps College Student Union Building in Jackson, the Junior Bar had offered the first of its "Young Lawyers' Seminars," which were intended to assist the neophyte attorney in making the difficult transition from the theoretical world of law school to the real world of actual legal practice. Lectures, together with printed subject outlines and forms, were given by outstanding senior mem-

6. Program of the 1935 annual meeting (Department of Archives and History, Jackson). State Bar records.

7. In 1973 the first volume of the *Journal of Space Law* was published by the University of Mississippi Law School.

bers of the Bar including Curtis E. Coker of Jackson, John A. Travis, Jr. of Jackson, Tom Leslie Darden of New Albany, and Russell D. Moore of Jackson.

Thirteen years later President Bacon told the 1971 annual meeting about a new program worked out by the law school liaison committee which would enable law students to gain some practical experience before they graduated through an internship program. Noah S. Sweat, Jr. had resigned his first circuit judgeship to join the University of Mississippi law faculty as director of the program. During 1970–71 several senior law students had worked in prosecuting attorneys' offices around the state, and it was hoped that the program could be expanded. The 1971 Legislature had passed the Legal Intern Limited Practice Act, which allowed interns to do courtroom work under the supervision of an experienced attorney, and in 1972 another act was passed which would allow "a senior law student intern [to] assist any public official in the performance of his official duties."[8]

Meanwhile attorneys already practicing were being offered a broader range of opportunities to increase their legal learning and to keep up with the latest developments by the inauguration of the "Continuing Legal Education Program" operated by the State Bar in cooperation with the University of Mississippi Law School. Plans for the program had first been formulated in 1962–63 under President C. Sidney Carleton; however, as Edward J. Currie, Sr. of Hattiesburg explained to the 1964 annual meeting, the turmoil over the integration of the University that year had delayed its implementation. On July 15, 1964, the Board of Commissioners finally authorized execution of the CLEP contract with University officials. Parham H. Williams, Jr. of Lexington, formerly district attorney for the fourth district, was to have joined the law school faculty as directors of the program, but, because he had the opportunity to go to Yale that year on a Sterling fellowship, he was replaced at the last moment by Luther L. McDougal III. McDougal was assisted by a Policy Committee chaired by Warren V. Ludlan

8. *Miss. Laws* (1971), c. 466; (1972), c. 415.

of Jackson and R. Pearse Phillips of Brookhaven together with law school professors John H. Fox, Jr. and Kenneth Vinson. In its very first year, in co-operation with several Bar committees, CLEP presented eight seminars around the state, most of them in at least two cities.

In practice, however, it proved difficult to operate the seminars from north-central Mississippi when most of the centers of population were in the central and southern parts of the state. Also the law school with its limited budget found difficulty in sparing faculty members from their regular teaching duties to participate in them. In 1966, therefore, the Commissioners decided to move the headquarters of the program to Jackson and place it under the supervision of the State Bar's new executive director, George Van Zant. Meanwhile, in 1965, the Conference of Local Bar Associations ceased its operations. CLEP and the Mississippi Bar Foundation between them had taken over most of its functions in keeping lawyers updated and in public relations on behalf of the Bar.

In addition to its concern for further educating its own members, the Mississippi State Bar has also always been concerned to educate the general public in the importance of a sound legal system and the benefits that come from living under the rule of law. One major means of doing so, much emphasized in recent years, has been the celebration of Law Day in May of each year. In 1969 and 1970 Mississippi's Law Day observances won national awards.

For the people to have respect for the law, of course, they must have respect for and trust in lawyers. So the work of the Complaints and the Ethics committees of the Mississippi State Bar has continued to be of paramount importance in recent decades. In 1962–63 the Ethics Committee was especially active. Meeting in Jackson on November 20, 1962, the members decided "to render written opinions concerning the most important and most prevalent unethical practices." Eleven such opinions were set down in writing at that same meeting, a twelfth in December, 1966, and nine more in March and December, 1968. As of April 2, 1976, the Ethics Committee had rendered a total of thirty-six written opinions for the guidance of Mississippi's attorneys.

The "Ethics Opinions" were published in 1976 in a booklet together with the "Code of Judicial Conduct" adopted by the Mississippi Conference of Judges at a meeting in October, 1974, and the "Code of Professional Responsibility," which contained the latest in the series of canons of ethics adopted by the Mississippi State Bar throughout its history. The new code was originally drafted by the 1970–71 Ethics Committee chaired by Presiding Justice Robert G. Gillespie of the state Supreme Court. Like its predecessors it was meant to comply with the ethical canons of the A.B.A., a new set of which had recently been promulgated; thus at the 1970 annual meeting A.B.A. president-elect Edward L. Wright of Little Rock was invited to lead a panel discussion on the national group's new rules. After a few further months of study the committee recommended to the Board of Commissioners that the Mississippi Bar adopt the A.B.A. canons with only a few minor changes. The Board agreed and sent the draft code to the Supreme Court who gave it their formal approval on March 15, 1971. By the time of the 1971 annual meeting President Bacon was able to report that copies of the new rules of professional conduct had been mailed out to every lawyer in the state.

In his speech Bacon suggested that confidence in the legal profession could be further strengthened if the State Bar would create a fund from which persons who had lost money because of a lawyer's dishonesty could be refunded. The idea was well received by members, and on February 19, 1972, the Commissioners, meeting on the University of Mississippi campus, gave their final approval to the establishment of the "client security fund."[9]

Responsibility for initiating disciplinary proceedings against the tiny handful of Mississippi lawyers guilty of unethical conduct since 1956 has rested with the Complaints Committee. In 1974 a new state law was passed which gave statutory recognition to the committee and laid down precise procedural rules for inquiring into accusations of improper professional conduct by an attorney. Whenever the Complaints Committee considered that a complaint

9. Commissioners' Minutes.

lodged with them might have some validity, it was to be investigated by a "complaint counsel" retained by the State Bar. After hearing the complaint counsel's report, the committee, when the circumstances justified it, could either reprimand the offending attorney itself, or, in serious cases, lodge a complaint against him in the name of the State Bar before the Supreme Court. The chief justice was then to appoint a "complaint tribunal" consisting of attorneys from the two Supreme Court districts other than the one in which the accused resided and did business. The tribunal's responsibility would be to meet in the accused's home county and there conduct "a full evidentiary hearing on an adversary basis." After hearing the evidence, the tribunal members could exonerate the attorney, reprimand him, recommend his suspension for a specific period of time, or recommend his disbarment. Unless the attorney appealed the tribunal's decision to the Supreme Court within thirty days, the decision would be final. A suspended attorney would have to pay a fine of $250 at the end of his period of suspension in order to be readmitted to practice. A disbarred attorney would not be eligible for readmission for three years and, if readmitted, would have to pay a $500 fine.[10]

But, while getting rid of the few dishonest or unprincipled attorneys is very important, the standards for admission to the Bar have the greatest effect on the overall quality of the legal profession in Mississippi. In 1954 the Legislature finally did enact most of the measures that had been included in the State Bar's draft act of 1947. After several decades of controversy, the 1954 statute at last imposed a minimum requirement of at least two years of undergraduate college education followed by at least two years of training either in an accredited law school or as an apprentice in an approved law office before the Bar Exam could be taken. Rejected, however, was the suggestion for a Board of Bar Examiners consisting of a Supreme Court justice, a practicing attorney from each of the Supreme Court districts, and the dean or some other faculty member from the University Law School. Instead the Board

10. *Miss. Laws* (1974), c. 566.

would continue to be appointed by the governor, but now from a list of eighteen nominees submitted by the Supreme Court. The administration of the exam was entrusted to the secretary of the State Bar, and the bar was also to be required to meet the costs involved out of fees.[11] The authorized fee of $25 per candidate was never enough to cover the expenses, and in 1959 it was decided to ask the 1960 Legislature to raise it to $50. The legislators fortunately agreed to the request and also required out-of-state lawyers applying for a license to practice in Mississippi to pay $50 to the State Bar. By 1974 the fee had been increased a further threefold to $150, and the Legislature that year appropriated an additional $23,829 for the examining Board's operations.[12]

As of 1976 no other major changes with regard to admission requirements and procedures had been made. Although coming in for a great deal of criticism, the diploma privilege for University of Mississippi Law School graduates remained in effect. The residency requirement for candidates originally from out of state was lowered from one year to six months in 1974, however, and the same statute allowed the Board of Bar Examiners rather more discretion than they had enjoyed before with regard to the subjects for examination and related matters.[13]

Even though upholding high ethical and professional standards has always been important to the Mississippi State Bar, protecting the interests of its members, financially and in other respects, has also been a major consideration. Breed O. Mounger of Tylertown, in his presidential address to the 1959 annual meeting at Biloxi, remarked that, beginning with John Satterfield four years earlier, "the economic well-being of the Bar" had been a major concern of its officers. During 1958–59, he reported, a Lawyers' Business Affairs Committee had been hard at work compiling a law office manual that would soon be ready for distribution. It was not until a year later, however, in the summer of 1960, that a copy of *Fee*

11. *Ibid.* (1954), c. 213.
12. *Ibid.* (1960), cc. 286, 288, (1974), cc. 42, 510.
13. *Ibid.* (1974), c. 510. This was the statute that first formally recognized the title of "Executive Director of the Mississippi State Bar."

Computation and Law Office Management was sent out to every lawyer in the state. Made up in a looseleaf format, it could be updated from time to time by sending out new mailings.

However, ten years and a high rate of inflation had made the manual obsolete by 1970. That year President Boyce Holloman of Gulfport reported that an Economics of Law Practice Committee, chaired by Lester Sumners of New Albany, had conducted an exhaustive survey of the economic status of Mississippi lawyers by mailing out questionnaires to each member of the Bar. The results were being analyzed, with the kind assistance of the Research and Development Center in Jackson and the University of Mississippi's Computer Center. When the analysis was complete, it would be possible "to determine what lawyers are making in various parts of the state . . . and how they can increase their income. In addition we expect to develop a new suggested minimum fee schedule. . . ." A few months later the committee, chaired by Sherman Muths of Gulfport, sponsored a two-day seminar in Jackson on "Law Office Management." Conducted by Cullen Smith of Waco, Texas, the seminar, which was attended by 335 lawyers and legal secretaries, had as its theme "Practicing Law Profitably." During the summer of 1971, every lawyer in the state received a final report on the committee's findings, which was paid for by the Mississippi Valley Title Insurance Company. In 1975, however, the United States Supreme Court ruled in *Goldfarb et al.* v. *Virginia State Bar* that recommended fee schedules would no longer be allowed. So the Mississippi State Bar thereafter could no longer provide such a service for its members.

No doubt, however, it will continue to provide its members with group health and life insurance programs. Having such a program was originally discussed back in the 1920s, but nothing came of the idea at that time. The topic was not mentioned again at an annual meeting until 1951, when it was reported that the Commissioners had been looking into some group insurance possibilities. By 1954 group life and group health policies were available for members, and by 1956 both programs had attracted many subscribers who were grateful for the savings that they offered.

Judges, as well as lawyers, have money worries, and, because it is so important that the best-qualified persons not to be deterred by financial considerations from competing for judicial positions, the Mississippi State Bar has always been interested in judges' salaries. At the end of World War II lobbying by the State Bar had persuaded the 1946 Legislature to raise the annual salaries of chancellors and circuit court judges to $6,000.[14] By 1954, however, inflation had made that a ridiculously low rate for what were supposedly highly prestigious positions. At the annual meeting that year a draft bill was approved to raise their salaries to $9,000. And the extraordinary session of the Legislature held in September, 1954, mainly to react to the United States Supreme Court's *Brown* decision, demonstrated that it still had nothing but respect for Mississippi judges by passing the bill as it had been written. While that success was being celebrated at the 1955 meeting, it was remarked that the justices of the Mississippi Supreme Court had not received any raises for a long time and were in danger of falling behind. After five years of lobbying, the 1960 Legislature finally agreed to raise the Supreme Court chief justice's salary to $16,000, that of the presiding justice to $15,500, and those of the other justices to $15,000. In the same session all of the state's judges were granted additional retirement benefits.[15]

During the next decade inflation continued steadily to eat away at recent gains, however, and Bar resolutions supporting judicial salary increases again were frequently made. In 1966 the Bar prepared another draft bill to give the Supreme Court justices an extra $4,000 each and to raise chancellors and circuit judges to $16,000; it received legislative approval. Just four years later, as the result of lobbying by a committee of Bar past presidents appointed by President Holloman, the 1970 Legislature raised the Supreme Court justices by another $7,000 and the chancellors and circuit

14. *Ibid.* (1946), c. 275. The Bar had recommended, however, that Supreme Court justices be raised to $10,000 and chancellors and circuit judges $7,500.

15. *Ibid.* (1954–ext.), c. 16, (1960), cc. 335, 453. In 1952 the number of Supreme Court justices had been raised to nine and their salaries raised to $10,000. See *ibid.* (1952), cc. 244, 245.

judges by $6,000. Also, the salaries of county court judges were raised at that time to $13,500. By the early seventies, therefore, Mississippi's judges were being paid some three times as much as they or their predecessors had been receiving twenty years earlier, mainly due to the efforts of the Mississippi State Bar.[16]

The Bar's concern for adequate judicial salaries was but a part of their general concern for the caliber of the judiciary and the quality of the justice administered in Mississippi's courts. During the fifties and sixties a majority of the members continued to believe that the most valuable innovative reform that could be effected would be the creation of a Judicial Council such as already existed in many other states. Undeterred by earlier failures, they resolved at the 1953 annual meeting to try again in the 1954 legislative session. Attempting to answer some of the most commonly heard objections they stressed that (1) the Council would not infringe on the prerogatives of the Legislature because any new rules it proposed, under section 3 of the draft act, would have to be passed on by both houses who could, as they chose, approve, reject, amend, or add to them; (2) continuity on the Council would be ensured by section 4 which provided for the members to serve staggered terms; and (3) the Council plan did not represent "an attempt to slip over the lawyers of Mississippi the Federal Rules of Civil Procedure" because nine practicing attorneys from around the state would be sitting on the Council, any rules it formulated would require both Supreme Court and legislative approval before being put into effect, and anyway not all of the Federal Rules were even applicable to Mississippi practice. The members of the Legislature in 1954 were not won over, however. And although again in 1955 and 1956 the annual meetings of the Bar called for the setting up of the Council, their petitions were to no avail.

Ten years later the issue was still alive. At the 1966 annual meeting Chief Justice Ethridge observed in the panel discussion on "Improving the Machinery of Justice" that up to that date all of the "Bar's recommendations [had] been ignored, although at the

16. *Ibid.* (1966), c. 445; (1970), c. 402.

last session a subcommittee of the House Judiciary Committee evidenced some initial interest in it." Nevertheless, Ethridge was convinced, "Mississippi needs a Judicial Council," and he called for a campaign to bring one into being by means of a constitutional amendment. But if a majority of the Bar wanted it, a majority of the politicians remained adamantly opposed. Like Chief Justice Smith's "General Court of Judicature," the Judicial Council apparently was never to become a reality.

On the positive side, however, the Legislature was persuaded to lighten the workload of the Supreme Court by a 1976 statute which authorized the justices to employ any chancellor or circuit judge who was willing as a "Supreme Court Commissioner . . . to aid and assist the said court in the performance of its duties."[17] And with regard to the federal judiciary in the state, one fortunate by-product of all the controversy and violence over school desegregation and civil rights in the sixties was that the state finally did get the additional federal judges she had been requesting for decades. In 1961 William H. Cox of Jackson joined Judge Sidney Mize to become the second judge in the southern district, and in July, 1968, Walter L. Nixon of Biloxi was appointed as a third judge together with Cox and Mize's successor, Dan M. Russell, Jr. of Bay St. Louis. In the northern federal district, meanwhile, Claude F. Clayton of Tupelo had succeeded Allen Cox in 1958. When Clayton was appointed to the United States Court of Appeals in 1967, he was succeeded in turn by Orma R. Smith, who was sworn in in August, 1968. Four months earlier, in April, 1968, William C. Keady of Greenville had been sworn in as a second northern district judge, so Mississippi had three more federal judges in 1968 than she had had in 1960.[18]

Keady's appointment in April, 1968, came at a time when, as president-elect, he was due, just two months later, to take over as president of the State Bar. In his place the members elected by acclamation Chester Curtis, who therefore had to take on all the

17. *Ibid.* (1976), c. 305.
18. Frank E. Everett, Jr., *Federal Judges in Mississippi, 1818–1968*, (Vicksburg: n.p., 1968), pp. 139–42.

responsibilities of office without having first had a chance to acquire some experience as president-elect. Fortunately, however, his immediate predecessor, Webb Overstreet, was right at hand in Jackson to assist him in settling in to his duties. "I shall always be grateful for [Overstreet's] help and assistance," Curtis told the 1969 meeting, "and I wish to state that the momentum of his regime has carried forward into this year and without it this year's bar program would have suffered."

Besides gaining three more federal district judges, no doubt due in part at least to the influence of Senator James Eastland who became Chairman of the Judiciary Committee of the United States Senate in 1956, Mississippi continued to be represented on the Fifth Circuit Court of Appeals. In 1955 Benjamin F. Cameron of Meridian took the place on the court left vacant by the resignation of Edwin R. Holmes of Yazoo City, and, after Cameron's death in 1964, his place was filled a year later by former Mississippi governor James P. Coleman of Ackerman.

Occupying the bottom rung of the judicial ladder in the state, the justices of the peace, although their office is an old and venerable one with origins in late-medieval England, in twentieth century Mississippi and indeed throughout the United States had come to be regarded with a certain amount of suspicion and disfavor by the legal profession because of their lack of any legal training. In 1955 President Bob Farley told the annual meeting that the A.B.A. had adopted the policy: "If we can't abolish Justices of the Peace, then the next best thing is to attempt to educate them along the nature of their representation of the law." During the preceding year the University of Mississippi Law School in conjunction with the A.B.A., Northwestern University, the Municipal Officers Association, and the Mississippi State Bar, had sponsored the first of what were to be a regular series of "traffic court conferences" for J.P.'s. Conduct of the subsequent conferences was taken over by the Junior Bar Section, whose 1964 report indicates that there were problems in persuading justices to attend them since they were purely voluntary. The 1964 Legislature, however, made it mandatory for all newly-elected J.P.'s, before they could be sworn in, to attend a training course of not less than eighteen hours duration approved by the attorney general.[19] By 1970 the course was being given by the newly-established Mississippi Judicial College.

In the field of law reform undoubtedly the major legislative achievement of the Mississippi State Bar in recent years was securing passage by the Legislature of the Uniform Commercial Code (U.C.C.). Aimed at clarifying and updating most of the old laws concerning sales, bills and notes, warehousing, bills of lading, and secured transactions, it was compiled by a team headed by Professor Karl Llewellyn of the University of Chicago law school for the National Conference of Commissioners on Uniform State Laws and was completed in 1952 after ten years of work.[20] Described as "the most ambitious project yet undertaken by . . . the Commissioners," the Code was adopted first by Pennsylvania in 1953. That same year President Hafter appointed a committee to study its applicability to Mississippi. At the 1954 annual meeting the committee reported that, although Pennsylvania jurists appeared to be satisfied with the U.C.C., the Mississippi Bar would probably be well-advised to wait until it had been tried out, amended, and revised in such major commercial states as New York, Illinois, and California before trying to sell it to the Legislature.

All around the United States acceptance of the U.C.C. was generally slow in coming. In 1957 Massachusetts became the second state to adopt it. Only then did other states begin to follow. In 1959–60 President Clayton had another committee study the matter, and, after hearing its report, the 1960 meeting passed a resolution endorsing the concept of the U.C.C. and calling on the newly-elected Legislature to appoint a recess study committee to consider it in conjunction with the State Bar's committee. The legislators took no action immediately, however, so at the 1961 meeting the suggestion was repeated. That fall the Bar's U.C.C. committee decided to lobby the Legislature for actual adoption of the U.C.C. in

19. *Miss. Laws* (1964), cc. 330–31.

20. Friedman, pp. 581–82. Barnard Schwarz, *The Law in America* (New York: McGraw Hill, 1974), pp. 210–11. *Directory of American Scholars* (1957), III, s.v. Llewelyn, Karl N.

1962, and to help pave the way a study as to how the Mississippi Code would be affected by its adoption, financed jointly by the State Bar and the University of Mississippi Law School, was conducted by a team of law school students. Although the 1962 Senate was persuaded to approve the Code, it ran into serious opposition in the House; so its backers there, in order to save it from defeat, conducted a successful campaign to get it sent back to the Senate for reconsideration. The 1964 Legislature was in a conservative mood and had too many other problems that had to be faced; so it was not until 1966 that Mississippi finally became the forty-fifth state to adopt the U.C.C. By that time the State Bar had succeeded in persuading the Mississippi Economic Council, the Mississippi Bankers Association, the Mississippi Manufacturers Association, and other influential and concerned groups to support the measure, and its adoption was easily secured.

Next to winning acceptance of the U.C.C. by the Legislature, probably the second major achievement was securing from the Legislature in 1970 authorization for preparation of the new state Code, which was completed and approved in 1972. Major legislative successes, however, have been comparatively few in the history of the organized Bar in Mississippi in the twentieth century. Indeed a majority of the legislation called for through the years has been defeated. In 1952, four out of the sixteen measures sponsored by the State Bar were passed. In 1956, ten out of eighteen passed, though one was later vetoed by the governor. In 1958, the score was only six out of twenty-one, plus five out of fourteen amendments to the Code that were requested. A decade later President Overstreet reported that "some" of the forty bills lobbied for that year had been passed, and three years later President Holloman again reported success with "some." Passage of about a third to a half of the legislation asked for by the Bar seems to have been the average in recent decades. While passage of all, or at least a majority, would be much more gratifying, the rate of success actually compares quite favorably with the percentage of legislation of every kind that is passed out of all that is submitted.

As was the case with the U.C.C., energetic lobbying, combined with securing the support of other groups in the state that might be affected, appears to be the secret of success. The fate of the Judicial Council idea, however, shows that success can never be guaranteed. Laymen tend to mistrust changes in the law or in the court system that they do not understand, and some lawyers, including some who get elected to the Legislature, are very reluctant to allow any changes in the law as they learned it in law school years ago. All legislators, particularly in Mississippi, look with disfavor on any measure that might lessen the independence and power of their branch of the government.

Outside of the Legislature, among the people as a whole, the legal profession has always had to contend with the fact that down through history men have tended to resent a little, and to fear a little, those who work with the law because the law has such great power over their property, lives, and freedom. The feeling was there in the fifteenth century when Shakespeare's peasant rebel said: "The first thing we do, let's kill all the lawyers."[21] It was very strong, as Judge Truly noted, in America, including Mississippi, during the Great Depression of the 1930s; signs of it were manifest again in the "stagflation" era of the 1970s to the extent that the President of the United States could hope to raise his standing in the polls by denouncing bar associations in a speech as organizations that existed only to discourage reforms and keep lawyers rich. Presenting a united front is one form of defense against such populist attacks on the profession, of course. Governors Vardaman and Bilbo have been the state's two most outstanding populist leaders in the twentieth century, and it was not just by coincidence that the Mississippi State Bar Association was organized in 1906 against the background of the Vardaman administration and the Sandy Bayou affair, or that the Unified Bar Act was passed in 1932 immediately following Bilbo's second administration and the uncovering of the highway paving scandal. The best form of defense that the organized bar can present, however,

21. *King Henry VI*, pt. 2, IV:2.

is to enforce the highest possible standards of professional competence and ethical conduct.

But, even while withstanding occasional attacks from outside, the Mississippi State Bar (or, as many lawyers in the state—and the 1972 *Code*—call it, the "Mississippi Bar Association") has also had to cope with serious dangers and divisions within its ranks. Insufficient funds, before 1932 because of too few members and since then because of powerlessness to set their own dues, have usually been a major problem which prevented them from doing much that they would like to have done. It took decades before a really fair, efficient, and satisfactory set of procedures for disbarring dishonest attorneys was worked out. And even among the honest and well-meaning majority, there have been serious splits and differences. Until 1932 there was the basic division between the minority of lawyers who belonged to the Bar Association and the majority who did not. For more than twenty years within the "unified bar," the split continued between those who wanted no prerequisites for admission to practice but a sound moral character and passing the Bar Exam on the one hand and those who wished to raise the formal educational requirements on the other.

By the later 1960s, with the expansion and growth of the state's economy and a consequent trend to specialization by lawyers, a new split began to manifest itself between the "defense lawyers," who tended to be older, more conservative, pro-establishment, and A.B.A.-oriented, and the "plaintiffs' lawyers," who were apt to be younger, more liberally inclined, and associated with the American Trial Lawyers Association founded in 1946.[22] Happily the establishment of the Junior Bar Section in 1936, by giving younger lawyers a forum and an organization within the State Bar framework wherein they could speak and work for desired changes, forestalled the possibility of any really serious generation gap ever developing in the legal profession in Mississippi. If it had been al-

22. One symptom of the division during the past decade has been the founding of the Mississippi Defense Lawyers Association (1968) and the Mississippi Trial Lawyers Association (1976).

lowed to develop, such a gap would have become a very serious matter by the mid-1970s, because by that time almost half of all the lawyers in the state were in the "young lawyer" category.

By 1976 not only was there a larger number of young lawyers than ever before but also, among those young lawyers, a far higher percentage of women, who had always been welcomed and encouraged by the State Bar since its founding in 1906 but who tended until very recently to be discouraged by social pressure and custom from entering the legal profession, and a far, far higher percentage of blacks, who have had to struggle very hard in this century to gain acceptance in any of the learned professions. With such a high percentage of young members of both sexes and both races in its ranks, the legal profession in the state can face the uncertain future with all of the confidence of youth and with a greater capacity than ever before to understand and serve the needs of every kind of client. As for the older members, both those of them who have led and those who have only served in the ranks of the Mississippi State Bar, they can take pride in the fact that, in spite of all the dissensions, disappointments, and failures, as the organized Bar in Mississippi embarks on its fourth quarter-century the quality of legal training both before and after admission to practice, the quality of ethical standards enforced, the quality of the legal services provided to clients, and the quality of justice administered in the courts are all immeasurably better than they were in Mississippi three-quarters of a century ago. The "honor and dignity of the profession" have been more than maintained; they have been enhanced.

APPENDIX I

Presidents of the Mississippi Bar

G. D. Shands (January–June, 1906)
Murray F. Smith (June, 1906–07)
C. H. Alexander (1907–08)
J. S. Sexton (1908–09)
T. H. Somerville (1909–10)
W. H. Powell (1910–11)
A. F. Fox (1911–12)
R. N. Miller (1912–13)
Robert B. Mayes (1913–14)
Sydney Smith (1914–15)
R. B. Campbell (1915–16)
A. T. Stovall (1916–17)
A. A. Armistead (1917–18)
S. E. Travis (1918–19)
J. B. Harris (1919–20)
Gabe Jacobson (1920–21)
George J. Leftwich (1921–22)
J. B. Holden (1922–23)
R. H. Thompson (1923–24)
Stone Deavours (1924–25)
J. N. Flowers (1925–26)
D. W. Houston (1926–27)
R. E. Wilbourn (1927–28)
George W. Currie (1928–29)
T. C. Kimbrough (1929–30)
George H. Butler (1930–31)
W. W. Venable (1931–32)
Jeff Truly (1932–33)
J. H. Price (1933–34)
W. Calvin Wells (1934–35)
Frank E. Everett, Sr. (1935–36)
David E. Crawley (1936–37)
Marion W. Reily (1937–38)
R. M. Kelly (1938–39)
W. H. Watkins (1939–40)
W. E. Morse (1940–41)
Alexander Currie (1941–42)
Charles F. Engle (1942–43)
Ross R. Barnett (1943–44)
Bidwell Adam (1944–45)
Earle L. Wingo (1945–46)
R. C. Stovall (1946–47)
Stokes V. Robertson, Sr. (1947–48)
Phil Stone (1948–49)
Robert W. Thompson, Jr. (1949–50)
Gibson B. Witherspoon (1950–51)
Quitman Ross (1951–52)
Charles B. Snow (1952–53)
Jerome S. Hafter (1953–54)
Robert J. Farley (1954–55)
John C. Satterfield (1955–56)
M. M. Roberts (1956–57)
W. S. Henley (1957–58)
Breed O. Mounger (1958–59)
Hugh N. Clayton (1959–60)
David Cottrell, Jr. (1960–61)
Sherwood W. Wise (1961–62)

C. Sidney Carlton (1962–63)
Edward J. Currie (1963–64)
Earl T. Thomas (1964–65)
Orma R. Smith (1965–66)
John T. Armstrong (1966–67)
N. W. Overstreet, Jr. (1967–68)
Chester Curtis (1968–69)
Boyce Holloman (1969–70)
William A. Bacon (1970–71)
Lester Sumners (1971–72)
Tally D. Riddell (1972–73)
Joe H. Daniel (1973–74)
James H. Ray (1974–75)
Frank D. Montague, Jr. (1975–76)
Erskine W. Wells (1976–77)

APPENDIX **II**

The Original Constitution and By-Laws

(adopted at Jackson on January 25, 1906)

Name.

Article I. The name of this Association shall be the Mississippi State Bar Association.

Objects.

Article II. The objects of the Association are to foster legal science, maintain the honor and dignity of the profession of law, to cultivate professional ethics and social intercourse among its members, and to promote improvements in the law and the modes of its administration.

Election of Members.

Article III. Petitions for membership in this Association shall be addressed to the Chairman of the Board of Directors and indorsed by two members of this Association which Board shall consider the same, and report their recommendation to the Association at its annual meeting, to be held next thereafter. A favorable report by the Board of Directors shall entitle a person to membership without ballot, unless a ballot on such report is demanded by some member of the Association, and upon such ballot, five negative votes shall be sufficient to defeat any election for membership.

Membership.

Article IV. Any person shall be eligible to membership in this Association who shall be a member of the bar of this State, in good standing, and who shall also be nominated as herein provided.

Officers.

Article V. The officers of this Association shall consist of one president, three vice-presidents, a secretary and treasurer and a Board of Directors. One of the members of the Board of Director shall be its chairman. Each of these officers shall be elected at each annual meeting for the next ensuing year, but the same person shall not be elected president for two years in succession. All such elections shall be held by ballot. The secretary and treasurer shall be elected by the Board of Directors. The officers elected shall hold office until their successors are elected and qualified according to the constitution and by-laws.

Board of Directors.

Article VI. The Board of Directors shall consist of fifteen members, five from each Supreme Court district, and shall be, at all times, an advisory board for consultation and conference, when called out for that purpose by the president or any vice-president who may, for the time being, be acting as president.

Election of Members.

Article VII. All members of this convention enrolling themselves and all others who have requested their enrollment, and all persons elected as herein provided shall become members of the Association upon the payment of the admission fee as herein provided for. But after the adjournment of this convention all nominations for membership shall be made as herein provided.

Annual Dues.

Article VIII. Each member shall pay to the treasurer as annual dues, such sum as may be prescribed by the by-laws and no person shall be qualified to exercise any privileges of membership who is in default. Such dues shall be payable, and the payment thereof enforced as may be provided by the by-laws. Members shall be entitled to receive all publications of the Association free of charge. The admission fee shall be such sum as may be prescribed by the by-laws, to be paid as the member is elected. The admission fee shall be in lieu of all dues for the first year.

Adoption and Amendment of by-Laws.

Article IX. By-laws may be adopted or amended at any annual meeting of the Association by a majority of the members present.

Committees.

Article X. The following committees shall be annually appointed by the president for the year ensuing and shall consist of five members each:

1. On Jurisprudence and Law Reform.
2. On Judicial Administration and Remedial Procedure.
3. On Legal Education and Admission to the Bar.
4. On Publication.
5. On Grievances.
6. On Obituaries and Memorials.

A majority of those members of any committee who may be present at any meeting of such committee, shall constitute a quorum for the purpose of such meeting. Vacancies in any office provided for by the constitution shall be filled by appointment by the president, and the appointees shall hold office until the next meeting of the Association.

Duties of Directors.

Article XI. The Board of Directors shall perform such duties as may be assigned to them by the president, or as may be provided by the by-laws, except as herein otherwise directed.

Meeting of the Association.

Article XII. This Association shall meet annually at such times and place as it may select, and fifty members present at such meeting shall constitute a quorum. The secretary shall give sixty days' notice of time and place of such meeting, either by publication in a public newspaper or by personal communication.

Duties of the President.

Article XIII. The president shall open each annual meeting of the Association with an address, in which he shall communicate the most noteworthy changes in the statute law, on points of general interest, made in the state and by the Congress during the preceding year.

Alterations or Amendments of the Constitution.

Article XIV. This constitution may be altered or amended by a vote of three-fourths of the members present at any annual meeting, but no such change shall be made at any meeting at which less than fifty members are present.

Suspension of Members.

Article XV. Any member of the Association may be suspended or expelled for misconduct in his relations to this Association or in his profession, on conviction thereof, in such manner as may be prescribed by the by-laws.

BY-LAWS.

I. President.

The president shall preside at all meetings of the Association, and in case of absence, one of the vice-presidents shall preside.

II. Secretary and Treasurer.

The secretary and treasurer shall keep a record of all meetings of the Association, and of all other matters of which record shall be deemed advisable by the Association, and shall conduct the correspondence of the Association, with the concurrence of the president. He shall notify the officers and members of their election, and shall keep a roll of the members, and shall issue notices of all meetings; and shall collect, and, under the direction of the Board of Directors, disburse all funds of the Association. He shall report annually and oftener if required; he shall keep regular accounts, which shall be at all times open to the inspection of the members of the Association. His accounts shall be audited by the Board of Directors. Before discharging any of the duties of this office, the incumbent shall execute a bond with good and sufficient surety, to be approved by the president, payable to the president and his successors in office, in the sum of one thousand dollars, for the use of the Association, and conditioned that he will well and faithfully perform the duties of his office so long as he discharges any of the duties thereof.

III. Board of Directors.

The Board of Directors shall meet at least once every six months and oftener, if called together by the president or by the chairman. They shall have power to make such regulations, not inconsistent with the charter, constitution and by-laws, as shall be necessary for the protection of the property of the Association, and for the preservation of good order in the conduct of its affairs. They shall keep a record of their proceedings, which shall be read at the ensuing meeting of the Association, and it shall be their duty to present business for the Association. They shall have no power to make the Association liable for any debts amounting to more than half the amount in the treasurer's hand in cash, and not subject to prior liabilities. They shall perform such other duties as are required of them by the charter, constitution, or as may be assigned to them by the president.

IV. Order of Business.

At each annual, stated or adjourned meeting of the Association, the order of business shall be as follows:

1. Reading Minutes of Preceeding Meeting.
2. Address of President.

3. Report of the Secretary and Treasurer.
4. Report of Board of Directors.
5. Election, if any, to Membership.
6. Report of Standing Committees.
7. Report of Special Committees.
8. Miscellaneous Committees.
9. Miscellaneous Business.
10. Election of Delegates to American Bar Association.
11. Election of Officers.

The order of business may be changed by a vote of the majority of the members present.

No person in discussion shall occupy more than ten minutes at a time, nor be heard more than twice on the same subject.

The parliamentary rules and orders contained in Roberts' Rules of Order, except as otherwise herein provided, shall govern all meetings of the Association,

V. Members Elect.

If any person elected does not, within one month after notice of his election, signify his acceptance of membership by a letter to the secretary and treasurer to that effect, and by payment of his admission fee, he shall be deemed to have declined to become a member.

VI. Committees.

In pursuance of Article X, of the Constitution, there shall be the following standing committees:

1. A Committee on Jurisprudence and Law Reform, who shall be charged with the duty of attention to all proposed changes in the law, and of recommending such as, in their opinion, may be entitled to favorable consideration of the Association.

2. A Committee on Judicial Administration and Remedial Procedure, who shall be charged with the duty of the observation of the workings of our judicial system, the collection of information, the entertaining and examination of projects for a change or reform in the system, and of recommending from time to time to the Association such action as they may deem expedient.

3. A Committee on Legal Education and Admission to the Bar, who shall be charged with the duty of examining and reporting what change it is expedient to propose in the system and mode of legal education, and of admission to the practice of the profession in the State of Mississippi.

4. A Committee on Publication, who shall be charged with the duty of examining and reporting upon all matters proposed to be published by authority of the Association, and pertaining to any of the subjects for the advancement of which the Association is created.

5. A Committee on Grievances, who shall charged with the hearing of all complaints which may be made in matters affecting the interests of the legal profession and the practice of law, and the administration of justice, and to report the same to this Association with such recommendations as they may deem advisable; and said committee shall, in behalf of the Association, institute and carry on such proceedings against offenders, and to such extent as the Association may order, the cost of such proceedings to be paid by the treasurer on the warrant of the Board of Directors out of any moneys subject to be appropriated by them.

VII. Appointment.

Each of the standing committees shall consist of five members, and shall be appointed annually by the president of the Association, and shall continue in office until the annual meeting of the Association next after their appointmentl and until their successors are appointed, with power to adopt rules for their own government, not inconsistent with the charter, constitution or these by-laws. Any standing committee of the Association may, by rule, provide that three successive absences from the meetings of the committee, unexcused, shall be deemed a resignation by the member so absent from his place upon the Committee. Any standing committee of the Association may, by rule, impose upon its members a fine for non-attendance, and may provide for the disposition of the fines collected under such rule.

VIII. Charges Against Members.

Whenever any complaint shall be preferred against a member of the Association for misconduct in his relations to this Association, the member or members preferring such complaint shall present it to the Committee on Grievances, in writing, and subscribed by him or them, plainly stating the matter complained of, with particulars of time, place and circumstances. The committee shall carefully examine and consider the same after giving reasonable notice to the party against whom the complaint is made of the time and place of hearing and shall report to the Association at the next annual meeting, recommending what action it should take in the premises.

IX. Charges Against Lawyers and Judges.

All complaints which may be preferred against lawyers or judges, affecting their professional or official conduct, shall be enquired into and examined by the Committee on Grievances, on behalf of the Association, in such manner as may be authorized and prescribed by the laws of the State.

X. Nominations and Elections.

Nominations of candidates to fill the respective offices, except the office of secretary and treasurer, may be made at the time of election by any member, and as many candidates may be nominated for each office as members may wish to name, but all elections, whether to office or membership, must be by ballot. A majority of the votes cast shall be sufficient to elect to office, but five negative votes shall be sufficient to defeat an election to membership.

XI. Supplying Vacancies.

All vacancies in any office or committee of this Associa tion shall be filled by appointment of the president and the persons thus appointed shall hold for the unexpired term of his predecessor; but if a vacancy occur in the office of president, it shall be filled by the Association at its first stated meeting occurring more than ten days after the happening of such vacancy, and the person elected shall hold for the unexpired term of his predecessor.

XII. Annual Dues.

Each member shall pay to the secretary and treasurer of the Association, the sum of five dollars, as annual dues; and the admission fee of five dollars shall be paid to the secretary and treasurer, as a member is elected. All annual dues shall be paid on or before the first day of March in each year, and any member failing to pay his annual dues by that time shall be in default, provided ten days' notice thereof shall have been given him by the secretary and treasurer; and upon the order of the president, the secretary and treasurer shall strike the name of such member from the rolls of membership, unless for good cause shown, the president shall excuse such default, in which last event the name of such member shall, upon the order of the president be restored by the secretary and treasurer to the roll of membership.

XIII. Amendment of By-Laws.

These by-laws may be amended at any stated, adjourned or annual meeting of the Association by a majority of those present.

XIV. Resignation of Officers and Members.

Any officer may resign at any time upon settling his accounts with the Association. A member may resign at any time upon the payment of all dues to the Association; and from the date of the receipt by the secretary and treasurer of a notice of resignation, provided that all dues have been paid, the person giving such notice shall cease to be a member of the Association.

XV. Salary of Secretary and Treasurer.

The annual salary of the secretary and treasurer shall be three hundred dollars, one-half of which shall be due on the first day of May, and the other half on the first day of November in each year, but may be paid earlier, or at other times if the Board of Directors, shall, in writing, so direct; but this shall be in full of all compensation to him. No other officer of the Association shall receive any salary or compensation.

XVI. Special Meetings.

If the president and Board of Directors shall determine that it is necessary for the Association to hold any other meeting during the year than the regular annual meeting, the same shall be held at such time and place as the president and Board of Directors may fix, upon twenty days' notice of such time and place, to be given by the secretary and treasurer by publication in a newspaper and notice thereof to each member; and the secretary and treasurer shall give this notice upon order of the president.

XVII. Honorary Members.

All Judges of the Supreme, Circuit and Chancery Court of this State and the United States Judge for the two districts of this State are honorary members of this Association, and they are relieved from the payment of admission fees and dues.

XVIII. Certificate of Membership.

A certificate of membership shall be issued to each member of this Association upon his election and payment of initiation fee, which certificate shall be signed by the president and secretary.

XIX.

The annual meeting of the Association shall be held on the first Tuesday after first Monday of May of each year.

Adopted May 9th, 1907.

Index